The Senses of Preaching

Thomas G. Long

John Knox Press
ATLANTA

Library of Congress Cataloging in Publication Data

Long, Thomas G., 1946–
    The senses of preaching.

    Bibliography: p.
    1. Preaching.   I.   Title.
BV4211.2.L66   1988   251   88–9148
ISBN 0–8042–1570–7 (pbk.)

© copyright John Knox Press 1988
10 9 8 7 6 5 4 3 2 1
Printed in the United States of America
John Knox Press
Atlanta, Georgia 30365

Acknowledgement is made for permission to quote from the following sources:

To Abingdon Press for excerpt from *Sermons for the Celebration of the Christian Year* by Vance Barron, published by Abingdon Press, © 1977.

To C.S.S. Publishing Company for excerpts from *Shepherds and Bathrobes* by Thomas G. Long. Copyright © 1987 by C.S.S. Press.

To Doubleday for excerpt from *The Diary of a Country Priest* by Georges Bernanos. Copyright © 1974 by Doubleday and Company.

To Fortress Press for excerpts from *Why Preach? Why Listen?* by William Muehl. Copyright © 1986 by Fortress Press.

To Harcourt Brace Jovanovich for excerpt from A GOOD MAN IS HARD TO FIND AND OTHER STORIES, copyright 1953 by Flannery O'Connor; renewed 1981 by Mrs. Regina O'Connor. Reprinted by permission of Harcourt Brace Jovanovich, Inc.

To Harper & Row for excerpt from *Dogmatics in Outline* by Karl Barth. Copyright by Philosophical Library Inc. Reprinted with permission of Harper & Row. For excerpt from *The Word of God and the Word of Man* by Karl Barth. Copyright, 1928, by Sidney A. Weston. Copyright, 1956, 1957, by Douglas Horton. Reprinted with permission of Harper & Row. For excerpt from *Telling the Truth: The Gospel as Tragedy, Comedy, and Fairy Tale* by Frederick Buechner. Copyright © 1977 by Frederick Buechner. Reprinted with permission of Harper & Row. For excerpt from *Teaching a Stone to Talk* by Annie Dillard. Copyright © 1982 by Annie Dillard. Reprinted with permission of Harper & Row. For excerpt from *The Crucified God* by Jürgen Moltmann. Copyright © 1974 by SCM Press Ltd. Reprinted with permission of Harper & Row. For excerpt from *Building the Word* by J. Randall Nichols. Copyright © 1980 by J. Randall Nichols. Reprinted with permission of Harper & Row. For excerpt from *The Word God Sent* by Paul Scherer. Copyright © 1965 by Paul Scherer. Reprinted with permission of Harper & Row.

To *Journal for Preachers* for excerpts from Thomas G. Long, "The Easter Sermon," *Journal for Preachers*, volume 10, number 3, Easter, 1987.

To Judson Press for excerpt from *Proclaiming the Acceptable Year*, edited by Justo L. Gonzalez. Copyright © 1982 by Judson Press and used by permission of Judson Press.

To Alfred A. Knopf for excerpts from *Dinner at the Homesick Restaurant* by Anne Tyler. Copyright © 1982 by Alfred A. Knopf, Inc.

To Thomas Nelson Publishers for excerpt from *The Easter Message Today* by Leonhard Goppelt et al. Copyright © 1964 by Thomas Nelson and Sons and used by permission of Thomas Nelson and Sons.

Preface

A minister of the Word who writes about preaching writes as a
learner to other learners and like them . . . is haunted by the
sermon that no one is great enough to preach.

Robert E. C. Browne, *The Ministry of the Word* (Philadelphia:
Fortress Press, 1976), 15.

The goal of this book is to engage ministers in table talk
about one of the most important aspects of our mutual ministry:
preaching. Much of the material in these pages was developed
for the 1987 Smythe Lectures at Columbia Theological Seminary,
and the conversational character of those lectures can still be
felt, I hope, in the present prose form. If the reader discovers
places in these chapters where he or she wishes to enter into dia-
logue, or even to make a rebuttal, then one of the primary pur-
poses of the book will have been achieved.

Although many practical suggestions are made here about
the craft of preaching, this is not intended as a basic textbook in homiletics. Even though the theological character of

preaching receives emphasis throughout, the reader will need
to look elsewhere for a full treatment of the theology of preaching. What the reader can expect is a wide-ranging, collegial ex-
ploration of some critical issues in the art of preaching, written,
to borrow Robert Browne's phrase, by one learner for other
learners.

I am grateful to the faculty of Columbia Theological Seminary and to President-emeritus J. Davison Philips, not only for
the invitation which set this project in motion, but also for the
many ways in which my colleagues supported and stretched me
during the five years I served on that faculty. I am also in debt
to those who listened so thoughtfully to my ideas when they
were given in the original lecture format and who responded
with many constructive suggestions for improvement. What is
written here is stronger because of their kindness.

Thomas G. Long

Contents

For Sherrill, Melanie, and David—my treasures

Chapter 1

The Eyes of Preaching

One cold December day I was reminded of a truth about preaching which I know and stand ready to affirm, but which every now and then disappears from my view. It was a Saturday. The lights and tinsel of Christmas were everywhere, our tree—just decorated the night before—was blinking away, and the Ray Coniff singers were chirping out "It Came Upon a Midnight Clear" over the radio. "For lo, the days are hastening on," they sang, and at that very moment I was involved in some intense negotiations with our teenaged son and daughter. They were reminding me that the days were indeed hastening on—only twelve more shopping days left—and that they had hardly made a dent in their gift lists. The best bargains, they were saying, are in New York City; "Please take us to New York."

So, compelled and propelled by a combination of guilt, responsibility, dedication, and the sheer bewilderment which comes with being the father of adolescents, I agreed to take them and their friends, six teenagers in all, on a shopping trip to New York.

We parked on the Manhattan end of the Lincoln Tunnel and walked up Forty-second Street to Times Square. If you have walked up Forty-second Street recently, then you must surely know what was happening in my soul as we marched through that shopping mall of the libido. Kierkegaard once said that "purity of heart is to will one thing." Forty-second Street seems to will one thing, all right, but I do not think it has to do with purity of heart. There they were, six kids marching up through the sleaze of Forty-second Street, wide-eyed with curiosity and wonder, yet trying their best to appear cool and nonchalant.

My son, my daughter—my treasures—being beckoned by the dope dealers, the hustlers, the porno queens, who were, it suddenly occurred to me, someone else's sons and daughters. Surely, at least for a moment, they had been, and perhaps were even still, someone else's treasures.

Anyway, we arrived at Times Square, and I asked them where they wanted to go. One of my daughter's friends smacked her gum and said, "Bloomie's." I gave them the directions, and off went the girls on their own to Bloomingdale's. My son announced that the boys wanted to look at cheap watches and radios, so I pointed my finger at the discount promised land, and off they went through the wilderness of jostling crowds, crack dealers, and street shell games.

For a moment I stood there all alone, wondering what in the name of God I had done. I had just turned six teenagers loose in New York City. Was I the mature parent, patiently building independence and responsibility in my children, carefully sizing up the risks one has to take if those one loves are to be allowed to grow? Or was I clinically insane? Should I have been arrested on the spot by the Department of Social Services and taken to Bellevue for observation? Fortunately the day went well, all returned safely telling stories of wild beasts and angels, and the psychiatrists at Bellevue did not get a shot at a diagnosis.

That is not the point of all this, though. The point of all this is that just as I was anguishing about the risk I had taken, I heard the voice of a preacher. There behind me, on a Times Square street corner, was a preacher trying to proclaim the gospel. Some empty place within me told me that I needed to hear some gospel at that point, so I turned toward the voice.

His appearance was about what one would have anticipated. His eyes were searching wildly, his urgent voice screeching through a distorted five-watt amplifier, his hands beckoning to the crowds which passed his asphalt pulpit. His message was not entirely lucid, but even in its disconnections you could feel him trying to get his words around a text: "And the Word became flesh and dwelt among us, full of grace and truth. . . ."

Most people were, of course, passing him by. Some stopped for a brief and curious stare. I noticed that even the hired Santa Claus positioned several feet down the pavement paused to listen every now and then. A good many people smiled benevolently as they walked by, a few laughed out loud, and one person asked him what he was on, even though it was not yet the third hour. The preacher just kept saying, "And the Word became flesh and dwelt among us, full of grace and truth. . . ."

To be honest I, too, find such street preachers to be amusing curiosities and interesting sociological types, but I no longer laugh quite as easily and deeply as I once did. I do not know if anyone ever really listens to what they have to say, or even if these preachers would know how to respond if someone did take them seriously and pay attention to them. But I do believe they have at least this one value, and this is the truth about preaching of which I was reminded: they are *parables,* dramatic symbols, of what preaching is finally all about. That street preacher is more than an object of curiosity. He is a *brother* to everyone who has ever attempted to preach the gospel, for all of us, in our own ways, preach into the teeth of the same cultural mix he faced. The gospel that we and he preach is, at one and the same time, the word most urgently needed and the word most easily dismissed.

There he stood, amid every scam, come-on, and con game known to humanity, trying to get the attention of people who do not know whether Christmas has to do with Bethlehem or Bloomingdale's. There he stood on the bank of a river of humanity, trying to the best of his ability to toss lifelines to people who do not know they are drowning. Every now and then I am certain the pitch of his words struck a tuning fork of recognition—"Preach on, brother!" or a silent "amen"—creating a small island of encouragement, a delicate community of shared faith. But there among the tourists and the cabbies, the street slicks and the bargain-hunters, the Parthians, the Medes, the Elamites and visitors from Rome, the kids looking for cheap watches, and parents struggling with their decisions, he seemed to offer the least attractive option in town, for all he had was a five-watt amplifier and a single fragile word. "You are Somebody's treasure," he tried to tell us, "because the Word became flesh and dwelt among us, full of grace and truth. . . ."

This book is intended to be a conversation with preachers about the ministry of preaching, and the place to begin is by thinking about what can be called "the eyes of preaching"; what preachers can and should see. Before a preacher *says* something a preacher must *see* something. To be a preacher is to be called to be a *witness,* one who sees before speaking, one whose right to speak is created by what has been seen. Sometimes pulpits are used as lecterns, but that is not what they really are. A pulpit is not a lectern or a podium; it is a witness stand, and the preacher's task is to tell the truth, the whole truth, and nothing but the truth about what has been seen.

That is where I think the Times Square preacher helps us. He helps us to see something of the context in which preaching takes place and something of the radical character of preaching itself. In other words, he helps the eyes of preaching to see clearly what we are looking *at* when we are preaching. Now I know that it is unlikely that any reader of this book is a street preacher. We do not preach in Times Square; we preach in softly-lit sanctuaries. We do not beckon to strangers; we preach to people who have more or less volunteered to be there and who are more or less attentive to what we have to say. If anyone snickers at us, it is usually done politely and out of our hearing. The witnessing that we do sounds more like conversation around the table with those we love than it does the urgent call of the street evangelist.

And that is the way it should be. In a later chapter I will try to underline the importance of the fact that it is the *church* to whom most of our preaching is addressed and that this is a good thing. On the other hand, it is a potentially seductive and dangerous thing, too, if we allow the presence of a relatively accepting congregation to lead us to the conclusion that when we preach we are doing a socially-acceptable, culturally-compatible, universally-appreciated deed. If our vision is clear, we can perceive that our sanctuaries are situated in the middle of Times Square, and our voice competes there with many other voices smoother, stronger, and more attractive than ours. If our eyes do not see that, then it is but a short journey to the conclusion that the gospel is just one more cheerful good word among all the words that wish us well.

During my seminary days I worked briefly as an announcer at a radio station. I learned then the fairly obvious truth that radio stations are not independent sources of artistic creativity. They want to make money by pleasing listeners, and they choose their musical formats from a small set of packaged choices that have proven to be popular. Some are country, some are album rock, some are middle-of-the-road, and so on. In those days, one of these packaged formats was designed for those stations you hear in dentists' offices or elevators, and as background in candlelit, high-priced restaurants. This format had several names, but the one I thought described it best appeared in a broadcaster's magazine. There it was called the "least objectionable noise" format. In other words, it was not designed to do *anything* to you. It was, in fact, designed to please you in proportion to its ability *not* to do anything to you. The music on these stations was not intended to make you fall in love, think new thoughts, march off to war, hum along with the melody, rebel against your parents, or even pat your foot. It was designed to make your subconscious say, "Well, that's not so bad."

Preaching is always in danger of falling into the "least objectionable noise" format. Several decades ago Paul Scherer reminded and warned us:

> When preaching is understood to be what it properly is, it is

bound to take on the character of a radical transaction; simply because in no other way can it represent the essentially radical nature of the Christian gospel. There can be no toning down of the lively Word of a living God, no softening of the "note of austerity," that note which is the very signature of all truth.[1]

That Times Square preacher was out there risking and experiencing rejection. I do not want to speculate about the psychological reasons for that; I simply want to thank God that this kind of rejection does not happen to us weekly. I *also* want to recognize that if we ever forget that the gospel is eminently rejectable, and that the New Testament word for "witness" is also the word for "martyr," then we will have lost sight of what we are really doing and risking when we preach.

Now, I want to say quickly here that I do not have in mind the kind of radical preaching which is often advocated. Some people seem to assume that the only corrective to the kind of soft and culturally inoffensive preaching that goes on in many pulpits is to begin doing a kind of preaching that virtually guarantees rejection because it spends its time spanking the listeners for various social transgressions and then prescribing various bitter-tasting medicines to help them get over the disease of injustice. The preacher can then judge his or her effectiveness by the varying degrees of outrage created by telling bank clerks and office managers that they are really the world's oppressors and informing families saving money for a child's college education that they have been co-opted by a system of bourgeois values. This approach, however well intended, simply assumes that if the "least objectionable noise" is false, then the "most objectionable noise" must be true.

But the math here does not add up; not in the economy of the kingdom. It is true that the gospel makes radical ethical claims upon us, and "anyone who enters the kingdom does so violently." What creates the demand of the gospel, however, is not the shame of being caught, but the power of being caught up in the vision of the new possibilities for life created by the reign of God. People cannot be scolded into kingdom behavior, but if they catch the vision of the kingdom, they will give their souls to be a part of it. In other words, what makes the gospel offensive in the first place, what causes it to cut against the cultural grain, is not that its news is so harsh, but that its news is so good that if people really believe it they will begin to cut their ties with the powers and principalities that have supported them so long and, to all appearances, so well.

One of my colleagues, a sociologist of religion named Richard Fenn, has written an intriguing book entitled *Liturgies and Trials* about what it means to speak the language of the faith in a secular culture.[2] One of his points is that it is characteristic of the secular society in which we live to place people on perpetual trial. In other words, the people to whom we preach on Sunday are under cultural indictment. Think about it. High school seniors taking SAT tests, people applying for jobs, employees undergoing their yearly reviews, patients in a hospital waiting for test results, are all awaiting the verdicts in their trials. Therapists judge our lives as "mature" or "immature." Programs like Parent Effectiveness Training serve indirectly to call our styles of parenting into question. The ready availability of divorce places all marriages on trial with the ever-present possibility that spouses will be found wanting. Teenagers walking down Forty-second Street have their ability to be cool and nonchalant dragged swiftly into court. Magazine advertisements depicting slim, successful people squeezing evident joy out of life judge the mundanity of our relatively uneventful lives. We are, "out there," all of us, on trial by the culture.

In Anne Tyler's novel *Dinner at the Homesick Restaurant*, Pearl, an elderly and dying woman, is thinking about her failures as a mother. Her husband left her when the children were young, and none of her three children have turned out to be the adults she expected and hoped they would be. Jenny, her daughter, is "flippant"; Cody is prone to go into rages; and Ezra is unambitious. "She wondered," the narrator tells us,

> if her children blamed her for something. Sitting close at family gatherings . . . they tended to recall only poverty and

loneliness—toys she couldn't afford for them, parties where they weren't invited. Cody, in particular, referred continually to Pearl's short temper. . . . Honestly, she thought, wasn't there some statute of limitations here? When was he going to absolve her. He was middle-aged. He had no business holding her responsible any more.[3]

The powers and principalities place everyone on trial, and there is no statute of limitations. They placed the preacher on Times Square on trial, too, and for most who passed by, it was a swift trial. His testimony was deemed irrelevant, or at best, circumstantial. Mainly he was laughed out of court. His verdict? Guilty of inconsequence, or perhaps better, *nolo contendere,* no contest. Peter DeVries has a character in one of his novels who is pastor of the Church of the Unwarranted Assumption, and DeVries means, of course, to include all who minister in that title. We must not fail to see that we who preach are on trial in the courtroom of culture, and the jury is smiling at us because we are all, in their view, the pastors of the church of the Unwarranted Assumption.

Listen now to what Richard Fenn says about this:

No wonder that the biblical tradition names the devil as "the Accuser" and assigns to him jurisdiction over "the world" or the current aeon. It is only with the Day of the Lord that all accusation ends, and the trial is over.

It is for that reason on the Lord's Day that the people of God celebrate a mock trial, in which the law is read, confession and testimony obtained, and the verdict once again given as it was before all time.[4]

Fenn is saying that actually two public trials are going on simultaneously. In one, the powers and principalities have placed all of us on trial, a never-terminating trial of endless appeals. Will we measure up? Can we get our act together? Even the people of God, or maybe especially the people of God, are involved in this trial: "They will deliver you up to magistrates in my name." However, hidden from view, another trial is going on, and in this other trial, the powers and principalities themselves have been placed on trial by God. They do not see the courtroom, are not even aware that the trial is going on, but they are on trial nonetheless. And when the guilty verdict in this trial is pronounced upon the powers, all those who have been accused by them in the first trial are set free. As the old gospel folk song puts it, "All my trials, Lord, soon be over."

The eyes of preaching see that when we preach it looks like we are making a weak confession in the world's trial, when we are actually testifying in God's trial of the enslaving powers. What the Times Square preacher was doing that Saturday was what every faithful preacher does every Sunday. He was giving testimony to people who are under indictment in the world's trial, and, from the perspective of that trial his words were simply inadmissible evidence. What was hidden except to the eyes of faith, though, was that he was actually testifying in the other trial, praying that his frail words would be gathered up into a testimony to the Truth.

When I was a seminary student I spent part of my training in Atlanta working for the Community Relations Commission, a watchdog agency of the city government. My job was to slip unnoticed into the municipal courtrooms of the City of Atlanta and to observe what was occurring. My assignment was to determine whether the defendants in those courtrooms were being treated with respect and dignity or whether there was unequal treatment on the basis of race or social standing. I looked for this, but what struck me most was something else—in the criminal court, most of the people brought to trial are repeat offenders. Occasionally some socially respectable, reasonably well-to-do person would appear, but mainly I saw chronic petty thieves, frequent brawlers, and prostitutes arrested for the hundredth time.

Now, if I were hauled into court, my main concern would be whether I would be convicted or not, but that is not the question that hangs in the air in municipal court. A guilty verdict, for the most part, is a foregone conclusion, and the question there is not, "Will I be declared innocent?" but rather, "Who is the judge today?" Some are hanging judges and some are easier; the question of urgency is, "Who is the judge?"

What the Times Square preacher was trying to say out

there in the public courtroom was what he saw: that the chamber doors of the courtroom that really mattered had swung open and the judge who was emerging was not the robed representative of the powers and principalities, but Jesus Christ, who will come to judge the living and the dead.

Perhaps you know that powerful Declaration of Pardon which appears in the *Worshipbook* of the Presbyterians:

> Who is in a position to condemn? Only Christ, and Christ died for us, Christ rose for us, Christ reigns in power for us, Christ prays for us.
>
> Friends: Believe the good news of the gospel. In Jesus Christ we are [innocent].[5]

"Here is the final verdict," the preacher in Times Square told us. "You are God's treasure because the Word which finally judges us 'became flesh and dwelt among us, full of grace and truth.'"

What I am saying here about the eyes of preaching is that the very first thing that a preacher ought to see is the place where our preaching takes place. We should not let the stained glass and the organ pipes deceive us. They should orient us to the fact that our preaching takes place at the intersection of two trials. We preach to Caesar's subjects, but we give testimony in God's proceedings.

We can see the biblical evidence of this in the Gospel of John through the witness of John the Baptist, who was perhaps the first Times Square preacher in the gospels.[6] "This is the testimony of John," writes the evangelist. What had happened, as you know, is that officials had been sent from Jerusalem to gather evidence against John. He was on trial.

Just so, as soon as John had been placed under interrogation, he blurted out a confession. Strangely enough, it was a confession that belonged in another courtroom and was pertinent to another trial: "He confessed, he did not deny, but confessed, 'I am not the Christ'" (John 1:20). The authorities had come for an affidavit about John; John provides a testimony about the Christ. There are two trials going on here. The officials are conducting one; John insists upon being a witness in the other.

They attempt to put John to the test, but, ironically, his testimony turns the tables and places them on trial. Indeed, if we listen to the court record, we can hear the overlap of the two proceedings, feel the mounting frustration of the prosecutors as their key witness gives his deposition in a case they did not even know was being tried:

Prosecution:	What, then, are you Elijah?
John:	I am not.
Prosecution:	Are you the prophet?
John:	No.
Prosecution:	Who are you, then? Tell us about *yourself.* Answer the court.
John:	I can speak about myself only by speaking of someone else. I cry in the wilderness, announcing the coming of another.
Prosecution:	This is confusing. Why, then, are you baptizing?
John:	I baptize with water, but there is one standing in this court at this very moment, and you do not know him. I am not worthy to untie his sandals.

Back and forth it went, the questions and the answers, the authorities conducting one trial, John giving his witness in another, until finally we are left to wonder which trial is real. Is John the defendant, or are the officials? Is it John on trial, or is it the world?

The earliest Christians must have heard this story of John's interrogation with great enthusiasm, and perhaps even a measure of joyous laughter. They heard it as a story about the day they put old John the Baptist on trial, and he stood up and gave his witness to Jesus in a greater courtroom, one in which his accusers had no power. They also remembered the day they tried to put Jesus himself on the stand, the day they brought Jesus into court, and how he, too, turned the tables and put the accuser on the stand:

"Are you the King of the Jews?" said Pilate.

"Do *you* say this . . . ?" responded Jesus, turning his accuser into the defendant.

"*Me?* Am I a Jew?. . . . What have *you* done?"

"I bear witness to the truth. Everyone who is of the truth hears my voice."

"What is truth?" asked Pilate, convicting himself.

This ability to see how preaching is taking place out there in the public courtroom is, strangely enough, one of the reasons why homiletics has placed such emphasis recently on the power of what is traditionally called sermon illustrations. It used to be taught that illustrations do exactly what their name implies; they "illustrate" a truth in the sermon, make something clear, make something understandable, make something plain. Some illustrations in sermons, of course, still do just that. I like to call this type of illustration the "extrinsic analogy," because the preacher is trying to explain some concept and in order to do this finds some piece of experience that is like that concept and can, therefore, make it clear.

For example, I recently heard a preacher in a sermon trying to explain—of all things—the concept of eschatology, the idea that God's rule over the creation is already present but not yet fulfilled. Already, but not yet. That is a difficult theological concept to understand. What the preacher did was to talk about his boyhood memories of winter in North Dakota. The winters there were harsh and unrelenting, and they held great destructive power over the frozen land. In the town square of the little village where this preacher grew up, though, hung a thermometer, and as the weeks moved toward spring, everyone in town watched that thermometer. The first day the mercury rose to thirty-three degrees was a time of common joy, and the news was spread around town. Feet of snow still lay on the ground, and the winter had plenty of icy terrors left, but on the town square was a sign that the power of winter was already broken and that its strength was passing away. That is an extrinsic analogy, one which seeks to explain something.

But there is another kind of illustration in sermons, and for this kind the stakes are much higher. I call this one an intrinsic analogy, because the purpose here is not to tell some experience that is *like* the concept we are talking about in the sermon, but to tell some experience that is, in a small way, a part of the concept we are talking about. If we are talking about forgiveness, we need to tell some piece of experience in which there is forgiveness. If we speak of grace, then what is the experience of grace in the lives of ordinary people? These do not have to be the nice, packaged, preacher stories; in fact it is far better if they are not. We are trying to say what the Christian faith looks like when it is experienced by the couple on the front pew, the family mid-way back, the single person, the teenager in the balcony.

That is what makes this kind of illustration so important, because one thing the culture does to us is to delegitimize religious experience. The culture can explain religious experience psychologically, sociologically, and so on; in other words, put it on trial, find it guilty of exaggeration, and cut it down to proper size by reducing it to arbitrary categories. The use of human experience in sermons, then, does not just make something clear and plain; it stakes out the territory of genuine religious experience. It says, in effect, it *is* possible to experience the holy in the midst of life, and this is what it looks like when it happens.

Suppose we are trying, in a sermon, to speak about the theological issue of discerning our own sinfulness, of coming to an awareness of the destructive qualities which lie deep within our character. We do not need to explain this issue as much as we need to see how it comes to bear in the experiences of a person's life. Consider the following event which occurred in the life of ethicist Stanley Hauerwas:

> [This] story relates an incident between me and my father that occurred in an instant but has stayed with me for many years. In order to make it intelligible, I need to supply a little background.
> My father is a good but simple man. He was born on the

frontier and grew up herding cows. Living with a gun was and is as natural to him as living with an automobile is for me. He made his living, as his father and five brothers did, by laying brick. He spent his whole life working hard at honest labor. It would have simply been unthinkable for him to have done a job halfway. He is after all a craftsman.

I have no doubt that my father loves me deeply, but such love, as is often the case among Westerners, was seldom verbally or physically expressed. It was simply assumed in the day-to-day care involved in surviving. Love meant working hard enough to give me the opportunity to go to college so that I might have more opportunity than my parents had.

And go on I did in abstruse subjects like philosophy and theology. And the further I went the more unlike my parents I became. . . . I . . . learned that Christianity involved more than an admonition to live a decent life, which made belief in God at once more difficult and more easy. And I learned to appreciate art and music which simply did not exist for my parents.

Married to a woman my parents would always have difficulty understanding, I then made my way to Yale Divinity School, not to study for the ministry, but to study theology. During my second year in divinity school, every time we called home the primary news was about the gun on which my father was working. During the off months of the winter my father had undertaken to build a deer rifle. That meant everything from boring the barrel and setting the sight, to hand-carving the stock. I thought that was fine, since it certainly had nothing to do with me.

However, that summer my wife and I made our usual trip home and we had hardly entered the door when my father thrust the now completed gun into my hands. It was indeed a beautiful piece of craftsmanship. And I immediately allowed as such, but I was not content to stop there. Flushed with theories about the importance of truthfulness and the irrationality of our society's gun policy I said, "Of course you realize that it will not be long before we as a society are going to have to take all these things away from you people."

Morally what I said still seems to be exactly right as a social policy. But that I made such a statement in that context is surely one of the lowest points of my "moral development." . . . I was simply not morally mature enough to know how to respond properly when a precious gift was being made.

For what my father was saying, of course, was that some-
day this will be yours and it will be a sign of how much I cared
about you. But all I could see was a gun, and in the name of
moral righteousness, I callously rejected it.
. . . On the surface my response was morally exemplary.
. . . But in fact what I did was deeply dishonest, as it revealed a lack of self, the absence of a sustaining narrative sufficient to bind my past with my future.[7]

That story is an intrinsic analogy. It does not explain a
truth; it embodies it. Moreover, it does so in such a way that
those who hear it are prompted both to recall and to anticipate similar experiences in their own lives and to seek after a
moral and theological depth in them.

The eyes of preaching, then, see what preaching is all
about, how it is that preaching takes place at the crossroads
of two trials. But that is not all that preaching sees. We have
examined what preaching is looking *at;* another way to pose
the question of sight is to ask, "What are we looking *for* when
we preach?"

What are we looking *for* when we preach? Maybe the best
way for us to measure that quality is to ask ourselves, "What
comment would we most like to hear about our sermon at the
door of the church?"

We can deal quickly with the fact that most of us who
preach would like to hear a little genuine praise about our
preaching at the church door. Some famous Scottish preacher,
I am not sure which one, was reported to have said caustically
that American preachers go to the door to receive compli-
ments when they ought to go to the study and pray for forgiveness. Well, if any famous Scottish preacher ever really
said that, he can go to hell as far as I am concerned. In the
first place, a lot more pastoring than praising goes on at the
church door. Second, rushing to the study to beat one's breast,
crying "mea culpa" after an eighteen-minute sermon, seems to
me to be simply reverse arrogance, and it tries the patience of
God. And third, what is so wrong with hoping that a few people found what you had to say helpful? If praise is all we are
looking for, then God help us, our ministry is sick and corrupt,

but when a preacher who has put hours of work into creating a sermon that engagingly relates Bible and theology to the needs of the people encounters the thanksgiving of some of the hearers, then God be praised.

But beyond that—and this is the crucial question—beyond affirmation, what are we looking for when we preach? The well-known Lutheran preacher Edmund Steimle once remarked that the comment he most prized at the door was, "Pastor, how could you have known?" What Steimle meant by this, I think, was that effective preaching resulted when the preacher was thoroughly in touch with the needs and hungers of people. The sermon, then, would portray the human dilemma in such profound terms that the hearers would discover things brought to light they had thought were hidden away in the secret recesses of their hearts. One of the most terrifying words in Scripture is the word spoken by the bridegroom, who is the Lord, to the five foolish maidens in Jesus' parable of the Ten Maidens: "I do not know you." Steimle suggests that the best response to preaching comes when people discover in the words of the sermon that, in ways they never imagined, they are *known*.

That is surely a good thing about preaching, but is it enough? Is it sufficient in preaching simply to look for people to realize that they are understood? As a student of mine said recently, "I am in therapy with a counselor who believes in clarification. I now understand all my problems with great clarity, but I still don't know what to do about them."

Another suggestion about what we should look for was made by a homiletician who is a devotee of the narrative approach to preaching. He offered that what we should hope for at the door is for the hearers to finish the storytelling in the sermon by telling stories of their own. Sermons, in other words, are to be intentionally incomplete in some strategic way and should invite the hearers to make closure by supplying their own experiences.

This "storytelling at the door" is to be understood figuratively, of course, but I saw this in concrete action not long ago.

My family and I were worshiping together, and we were privileged to hear one of the finest sermons I have encountered in a long time. The sermon included a story about the preacher and his wife picking up their young son after an afternoon of play at a friend's house. As they rode home, the boy was uncharacteristically quiet and seemed troubled. The parents gently inquired of their son what could be wrong, but he did not seem to want to talk about it. The parents, growing worried, encouraged him to get what was bothering him off his chest. "It's about Martin," replied the boy, referring to his playmate of the day, "but I can't tell you about it." The parents looked at each other, raising their eyebrows in concern, and prodded the boy to reveal what had happened. Finally he spilled the beans, "Martin says he doesn't believe in God," and with that, the parents breathed a collective sigh of relief that the problem was only theological and not something else.

The sermon went on from there, but at the door my own son did a thing most unusual for him. He grasped the hand of the preacher and said, "That happened to me, too." The preacher looked quizzically at him, and my son proceeded to report an experience in which one of his own friends also claimed to be a secret atheist. As for the preacher, he was sensitive, attentive, pastoral, and, I think, pleased that the stone he had tossed into the congregational lake had rippled out to create the response of my son's own story. The sermon story intersects with the listener's story, goes the current homiletical jingle, and that was precisely what had happened with my son that day.

This, too, is a good thing for preaching to create at the door, but is reciprocal storytelling enough, either? Despite the widespread notion that narrative is the literary form *par excellence* of Christian faith, and the deserved popularity of preachers who are good storytellers, plenty of additional evidence claims that Christians do not live by stories alone and have never done so. There is a rhythm in the language of faith between narrative and discourse, between story and insight, which needs to be preserved. We can already see it at work in the New Testament. Luke, for example, tells us, "And he told them a parable, to the effect that they ought always to pray and not lose heart" (Luke 18:1). Or in Matthew, again in the Parable of the Ten Maidens, the story itself is told and then someone, probably the evangelist himself, adds, "Watch therefore, for you know neither the day nor the hour" (Matt. 25:13). In other words, here is the story, but here also is the insight, the point; here is what to do about it.

Additionally, it is important to note that the equation is not one insight to one story. Good stories generate many insights. But if we preach only the insights, we end up with a propositional and scholastic form of the faith. If we preach only the stories, we end up with hopeless ambiguity. The rhythm between them must be preserved.

The reason this is important to say, I think, is because we need to keep in perspective a certain trend in contemporary homiletics. You have read, I am sure, some contemporary book on preaching which states something like, "The value of storytelling to preaching is that it allows the hearer to experience the story-shaped world." I have even said things like that myself, and will no doubt say them again. In context, they are worth saying, but hanging out there all by themselves, such notions are nonsense at best and destructive at worst. The issue here is that Christians tell stories with more in mind than allowing people to experience some narrative world or calling forth similar stories from the listeners. When we preach we are looking for discipleship in the real world. Whatever we say in sermons, narrative or not, we say in order that people be equipped to do things like "pray and not lose heart."

Now, I think, we are getting closer to what it is that we ought to be looking *for* in preaching. It is right at this point that I have been helped by no less a figure than St. Augustine. Book Four of his *De Doctrina Christiana* is a manual for communicators of the Christian faith. It is, to put it another way, one of our very earliest homiletical textbooks. Augustine, as you know, had been schooled in the classical rhetoric of Cicero, but now, as a Christian, he stood at a critical distance from his secular training: close enough to use it, but far enough away not to let it overwhelm the higher claims of the gospel.

In this way Book Four is amusing: Augustine opens it by denying that he is going to talk about rhetoric. "Learn it in the secular schools if you want to know it," he says; then he proceeds to talk about rhetoric for the entire thirty-one chapters of the book. Notice the genius at work here in his method. By denying that this is a textbook on rhetoric, he sweeps the expected category out of the mind of the reader. We have here something new in literature, a textbook on speaking that is not about rhetoric. What is this book about then? Speaking the truth, says Augustine, is what this book is about, and Augustine goes directly to Scripture to find examples of the way Christian truth bodies itself forth in the world as speech. Then, lo and behold, some of the things Cicero taught him about rhetoric are found right there in the way Scripture is composed.

Do you see how important this method is? I wish all practical theologians would learn it. How many books on ministry have you read which seize lustfully some piece of pop psychological or sociological theory and then proceed to saw the arms and legs off theology to make it fit the theory. Not Augustine. Theology calls the shots, and secular theory is brought in only when it is beckoned by the need of faithful people to gain clarity. Secular rhetoric was after eloquence, pure and simple. "So, should preaching, too, be eloquent?" asks Augustine. Certainly! But preachers should not strive to be eloquent. They should rather strive to speak the truth, and when they do, eloquence will come as a servant so obedient he does not even have to be called.

What happens, then when preaching throws the party and rhetoric shows up? Augustine says this:

> He who seeks to teach in speech what is good . . . that is, to teach, to delight, and to persuade, should pray and strive that he be heard intelligently, willingly, and obediently.[8]

He cribbed that from Cicero, but no matter. Contained in that quotation is what Augustine thinks we should look for in preaching; in that sentence we discover what Augustine would like to hear at the door, and I believe he is correct. At the door of Augustine's parish, he would be pleased if people would say, "I learned something today; I was moved by what you said; and, I intend to do something about it."

This rhetorical formula from Augustine cuts through a lot of baloney about preaching. First of all, he makes it clear that the pulpit has a *teaching* responsibility. This cuts two ways. For those of us who have been timid about doing any teaching from the pulpit, preferring to leave that to the church school classroom, Augustine informs us that we have been falling down on the job.

I could cite many examples of this, but let me be content with one: the use of critical biblical scholarship in preaching. There is a widespread tendency among preachers to keep critical matters about Scripture hidden away in the study. Any minister who has graduated from a halfway decent seminary in the last forty years knows the value of at least historical criticism in the understanding of Scripture, not to mention literary criticism, sociological criticism, and the rest. Most of us use critically-informed commentaries in the preparation of our sermons, and gain much from them, but it is only rarely that the critical material makes its way overtly into the sermon itself.

Why? Well, some of us say, that is not our job, to let people in on all the critical machinery. We are preachers, not Bible professors, and we do not want to clutter our sermons with stuff about the synoptic problem or questions about how many Isaiahs there really were. Others of us are perhaps a bit more candid when we admit that we do not often mention the critical problems because of the potential they have to create mutiny on the part of congregations. It took us three years of seminary to understand these issues, but it would take our congregations only twenty minutes to decide that their pastors did not really believe the Bible.

I do not want to underestimate this problem. I know that there are indeed church members who have their pistols

cocked, ready to fire at the first whiff of modernism, but I do
not think that is the prevalent reality. American Christianity
is by and large fairly conservative, and it is conservative
about the Bible, but one way to see popular piety about the
Bible is as a heroic holding on to the specialness of this book
against historical and existential realities which can only appear as destructive because there is no other way to understand them.

Let me put this more simply and concretely. My first year
in the parish I had a vigorous discussion over lunch one day
with a bright and faithful elder, a Bible teacher of long standing, about the Book of Jonah. My position was that Jonah was
by far a richer treasure of God's wisdom for us if we viewed it
as a literary creation with a theological message and did not
expend a lot of energy insisting that ancient Ninevah was actually so big it took three days to cross it or speculating about
the possibilities of human survival inside the digestive tract
of a fish. He, on the other hand, was defending the literal fac-
ticity of Jonah. It was a friendly discussion, but a serious one,
and two things became clear to me. First, he was a literate,
well-informed man, and he admitted having to strain to ac-
cept some things in the Bible at face value. Second, he was
willing to put up with the strain because to do otherwise was
to endure a huge loss, the power of the Bible to speak in a
trustworthy manner to him.

I do not fault him; to the contrary, I admire him. I believe
that he was the victim of bad preaching, some of it my own.
We who had preached to him had placed him in the position of
not even being able to wonder about the relation of history to
Scripture, when, as a matter of fact he is a participant in a
theological tradition that has wrestled with that problem for
centuries. It is a big job, and I could not accomplish it in a single lunch, but if his pastor, who shared his conviction about
the trustworthiness of God's Word found in Scripture, could
show how thoughtful and critical reflection on the Scripture
could be instrumental in the discovery of that Word, it would
have been liberation for him. Our Protestant forebears placed

the Bible in the hands of the people in their own language. It is now our responsibility to teach the Bible in such a way that those people can receive its truth without having to sacrifice their creative intelligence to do so. "I learned something today" is a good word to look for at the door.

Augustine's word about teaching cuts in another direction as well. Some people relish the teaching role in preaching. They run series on the phrases in the Apostles' Creed and what Christians believe. They teach the Bible carefully, filling their sermons with information about first century Pharisaism and the actual dimensions of ancient Ninevah. Stewardship season brings homilies on the definition of the word "steward," and their congregations are well-informed about how many different Greek terms have been translated by the one English word "love." Their hearers can pronounce "soteriology" and when they read in the paper about the Vatican's stance toward liberation theology it rings a bell. These preachers see themselves, to use the old Presbyterian phrase, as "teaching elders," theologians in residence. To these among us, Augustine would say, "Yes, . . . but. . . ." Yes, we are to teach; that is work well done. But we do not teach because teaching is the goal; we teach because it is necessary for preachers to teach in order to accomplish something else. The pulpit is not a lectern; it is a witness stand, and the truth to which we testify demands more than learning.

So, where does preaching go from teaching? Augustine's next and middle term is "delight," a technical phrase from rhetoric meaning roughly the satisfying emotional response of listeners to what is said. "You touched me this morning," "I was on the edge of my pew," "I was deeply moved by the sermon," "Usually sermons bore me, but not *that* one," or my son's comment, "That reminded me of something that happened to me" are all expressions of "delight." This is an important concept, and modern homiletics has made much of it. Aided by contemporary psychology and communication theory we now know, perhaps even more clearly than Augustine did, how active the listeners are, or can be, during the preaching.

Preachers and listeners have different jobs, but they are working together as co-artists to create the sermon. We can design sermons that help this process, and we can design sermons that kill it. I want to say much more about that in, I hope, a practical way in the third chapter. At this point, I simply want to observe that it has been a tendency of American preaching, at least since the end of the nineteenth century, to let the process stop with delight. We say it in different ways—we want our sermons to be inspiring, touching, moving, involving, whatever—but what we mean is that, at the door, we are looking for some signal that the hearers have been emotionally fed by our sermons.

And, God knows, that is not a bad thing. A member of a pulpit committee called me recently practically begging for the names of ministers who can preach. "We've listened to over fifty sermon tapes," he reported, "and we're numb with tedium." As the country priest in Bernanos' novel puts it:

> My parish is bored stiff; no other word for it. Like so many others! . . . [T]he world is eaten up by boredom. . . . [Y]ou can't see it all at once. It is like dust. You go about and never notice, you breathe it in, you eat and drink it. It is sifted so fine it doesn't even grit on your teeth.[9]

It is not an easy thing to be lively and engaging in the pulpit, and a firm handclasp with a sincere "you touched me today" is a rare and welcome word.

Augustine warns us that delighting people is only a wayside chapel on our pilgrimage, though. It is not the goal of the journey. We teach, yes. We delight, yes. Some sermons will be mainly teaching sermons; others will aim more at the heart. But teaching and delighting are present only as means to Christian truth's greatest end: to persuade. Augustine does not mean the same thing by persuasion that Billy Graham does. Augustine has in mind a larger idea, namely discipleship, the obedient ethical response to the claims of the gospel.

In his most recent book, William Muehl of Yale tells about serving as a debate coach to a local chapter of the American

Association of Bankers. These bankers were responding to the renewed emphasis on the social responsibilities of business by meeting regularly to debate economic, social, and political issues. One night, after a vigorous debate on the nature and destiny of capitalism, Muehl found one of the participants, a middle-aged trust officer, a pillar of the church, waiting for Muehl at the elevator. The man had a problem on his mind.

"You know, Doc," he said, "I've always thought of myself as a religious man, and I take some kidding from my friends about my church activities. But tonight, when we were discussing some of the ethical problems of capitalism I suddenly realized that if I ever had to choose between capitalism and Christianity, I'd stick with capitalism. Am I going to Hell?"

Muehl goes on to caution against assuming that this was the voice of one more greedy materialist. "He was," he says,

> a man of limited means, and it was obvious to us both that his future held in store little more than another decade or so of anonymous service at a modest salary. His commitment to capitalism reflected no mere commitment to money per se. It sprang, rather, from an almost inarticulate, scarcely identified but deeply rooted feeling about human creativity in general and his own reason for being in particular. . . . He felt a *need* to be creative, a need which clearly outweighed his obviously sincere commitment to the Christian faith, as he understood it. And he clearly feared that the two might be incompatible.[10]

Whether Muehl properly understood that man, I do not know, but I believe he is correct about how the Christian faith has been communicated. People know in their bones that they cannot be fully human unless they are *doing* something that has meaning, freeing all of their energies in the service of some vision that has power, some community that nurtures that vision, and some task that makes a difference. We may think that the resistance we often encounter from people is a signal that they want to be left to their own devices, but if we imply in our preaching that all the gospel wants of their lives is the sincere saying of a creed, attendance at worship, and an

occasional work day at the church, then they will find some
other vision—positive thinking, capitalism, or whatever—that
will take them seriously and put them to work.

Visitors to European cathedrals are often confronted at
the door by an offering box. You will often see tourists fishing
out a few coins and dropping them in the box, almost as if this
were the price of admission to get in to see the sanctuary. In
Strasbourg Calvin also placed an alms box at the door of the
church, but the worshipers did not place money there to get *in*
to the church; they placed offerings there on the way out of
worship. Giving money to the poor was their first act of obedi-
ence to the Word they had received in worship. "I learned
something today. I was moved by what you said, and I intend
to do something about it." It is this for which the eyes of
preaching look.

If that is what the eyes of preaching see, then preaching
must find a voice to say something. And that will be our concern in the next chapter.

Chapter 2

The Voice of Preaching

In his book on preaching, Dean Leuking describes a *New Yorker* cartoon picturing a slightly sheepish preacher leaning over the pulpit and saying to the congregation, "It's been a very full week, so if anyone would like to throw out a scandal, funny anecdote, or current event, I'll wing it."[1]

Anyone who has preached regularly knows the truth hidden beneath that humor. The pastorate is a demanding calling, and the pulpit is an incessantly hungry place. Whoever first coined the phrase "an hour in the study for every minute in the pulpit" either never served a pastorate or, if he did, was surely admired by both of his members. Preaching every week absorbs creativity like a black hole absorbs energy, as Sunday follows Sunday at a relentless pace.

Not long ago I was reading the application of a man who had applied to the graduate program of the seminary where I teach. In his file was a letter of recommendation from one of his seminary professors. As I read the letter, I realized that this was one of those occasions in which the writer of the letter was struggling to find a way to be both kind and honest about a rather weak applicant, and what he came up with was, I think, ingenious. He wrote: "In class he is eager and friendly, but I must say that he speaks more often than he makes a contribution." When I read that I thought it was perhaps the best description of my parish preaching experience I had ever heard. "He speaks more often than he makes a contribution," because Sunday comes whether you have something to say or not. As Edmund Steimle once phrased it, "Preaching in the parish is hand-to-mouth."

The issue this raises has to do with "the voice of preaching." In other words, what to say—what to say week after week after week—what to say? Part of what I have to report will not be news to any working pastor, and that is that responsible preaching is exactly what it appears to be: hard work performed under pressure. In part the demands of weekly preaching simply place before us the fact that to be called to preach is to be called to a rigorous discipline. Being a pastor is different, of course, from being an academic theologian, but the pastor and the academic theologian share at least this one thing: they are both called to love God with the mind. In responsible preaching there is simply no substitute for reading, thinking, reflecting, exploring, gathering, digging, watching, and analyzing. No one preaches with ease. The kingdom of preaching is proclaimed, and everyone enters it violently, even those who proclaim it.

I once heard a systematic theologian assert that one of the implications of the doctrine of creation is that Christians are interested in *everything*. I do know that preachers are called to think theologically about everything of importance that impinges upon the lives of their people, from the latest incident in the Middle East to the last episode of the Cosby Show. This is hard mental work; there is no way around that, but it is what we are called to do. Some pastors, I am certain, have completely action-oriented ministries and think they are being current and on top of things when they drag various bits and pieces of undigested contemporary experience into the pulpit to liven up their sermons and make them "relevant," but that is a shortcircuit which finally leads nowhere. It is the interpenetration of the vision of our faith and the circumstances of our life. This is what we are after, and discovering

that is hard work. We preachers are simply going to have to
get over the notion that when we are studying and thinking
we are not doing ministry. In some ways those activities lie at
the heart of the ministry to which we are called.

Not only is this hard work, it is time-consuming work, and
that is where the discipline of planning is crucial if we are to
make the most of the time which can be squeezed from a busy
pastor's life. The slogan "an hour in the study for every
minute in the pulpit" is better than vice versa, I suppose, but
it is finally an unrealistic legalism. What we need are ways of
establishing a rhythm between the time spent in focused
study and the time spent doing the rest of the tasks of ministry, so that each feeds and reinforces the other.

There are, I am confident, ministers who plan their
preaching a year in advance, and I hold them in awe. The best
wisdom of research into human creativity, however, tells us
that about five or six creative projects like sermons are the
most we can dynamically work on at one time. That is not
very many, but it is still four or five more than most ministers
are now working on. What this advance preparation involves
is enough careful work on the biblical texts and theological issues to raise the basic questions and directions of the sermons. Then what we read, what we see, what we experience,
what we hear will galvanize to those sermon cores. I know
several ministers who keep a half dozen or so file folders on
their desks, one for each of the next few upcoming sermons.
Into each folder goes a sheet of exegetical, historical, and theological notes. This comes from jealously protected hard study
time. Every now and then, between phone calls or whatever,
these ministers take a few minutes to leaf through the folders, so that the key issues are always on their minds.
Gradually, clippings from the newspaper, paragraphs from
books, ideas which have come from pastoral contacts find
their way into the folders. One of these pastors has even iden-
tified those members of the congregation who are avid readers
and asked them to be on the lookout for particular kinds of
material. When it comes time to write the sermon, more often

than not, the folder in question has some good material in it. Then that one is retired, and a new folder takes its place in line. In summary, the sermons are being worked on all of the time.

Even so, there is no system, no scheme of planning, which will completely take the pressure off of weekly preaching. And we will never quite get over the feeling that "we speak more often than we make a contribution." Some weeks, of course, it all comes together. The pieces have all fit; we have got something important to say; we like the way we have decided to say it; and we go into the pulpit with the zest and confidence of a person with a good word to speak. Other weeks, though, it is more like, "Gold and silver have I none, but what I have I'll give you."

We tell ourselves several things about the rise and fall of our preaching. Sometimes we say that people learn to endure our failures and dry periods waiting for the successes and the oases. Maybe so, but that finally devalues the service of worship and places the whole burden on the sermon. Alternatively, we may say with amazement that the very sermons we consider to be mangy dogs are often received with gratitude and hosannas by somebody in the congregation. Well, by the grace of God, that is often true, too.

But I believe there is a deeper word for us about this. I think what we need to realize about the cycle of highs and lows in preaching, when they are experienced by a minister faithfully attempting to perform the ministry of preaching, is that they are an embodiment of the true nature of the Christian life. Week after week the people gather around the Word. What they hear sometimes is a preacher who vibrates with passion and excitement. What they hear other times is a preacher who is perplexed, dry as dust, struggling to get in touch with the vision, or trying to squeeze blood out of a stone. That is the way it is with sermons, and that is the way it is with Christian life, too. The ups and downs of preaching are a ritual enactment of the rhythms of the Christian life. We find a powerful witness to the faith in a congregation who experiences their minister struggling with preaching, sometime having much and sometime having little. When the sermon is rich and full, it is a banquet of grace. When the sermon is less than that, it is still, like manna, enough to go on.

Sometimes I think that those congregations wealthy enough to hire a polished preacher and acquire enough additional staff so that the preacher can have the luxury of doing nothing but preparing sermonic masterpieces are the saddest congregations of all. They are insuring themselves against the rough, dull, unfinished, unpolished sermon and thereby creating the illusion that the Christian faith, properly experienced, is an unbroken series of majestic peaks. That is simply not the truth.

So the first word for us is that discovering our voice in preaching, finding something to say, does not come from a set of techniques or getting hold of the right sermon-help resource, but rather from an ongoing process of reflection and study, which produces mixed yields.

Another part of finding our voice in preaching is learning to listen more attentively to the voice of the biblical text. Biblical texts have claims to make upon us, things they wish to say. As someone else has said, "Texts once were preaching, and they wish to be preaching again."

It is amazing how many of us, if someone were to ask us our view of biblical authority and inspiration, would articulate a dynamic view of the living and active biblical word. We would be full of ideas about how texts are always creatively engaging us with truths ever new. That is our official position, but in practice we look at a familiar text, like the "Prodigal Son," and we treat it as if it were a slightly senile dinner companion who tells the same story over and over again and never says anything new. We give the text a quick glance, maybe sneak a peak at a commentary or two just to make sure that what we have always thought that text was about is what it is about, and then stew about how to say the same old thing in some sparkling way.

I once attended a performance of the musical *The Cotton Patch Gospel*. This play is based upon Clarence Jordan's translation of the Gospel of Matthew into the language and society of rural Georgia. I saw it on one of the final nights of the run, and the cast seemed especially frisky. At one point in the script, Jesus, played by a young man named Tom Key, was delivering the Sermon on the Mount. He looked out at the audience, pointed dramatically at the blank auditorium wall, and said, "Look at the lilies of the field." Then he stopped, as if he had forgotten the next line. After a pause, he pointed again, "Look at the lilies of the field." He stopped again, and then, like a phonograph needle stuck in a groove, he repeated it, "Look at the lilies of the field." The audience began to shift with a little discomfort, but then Key turned to the rest of the cast on the stage, shrugged his shoulders and said, "I can't get them to look." We laughed with relief and with the awareness that he was talking about *us*, and when he said again, "Look at the lilies of the field," every head in the house turned toward that blank wall.[2]

Not a bad word for preachers there. Look—really look at the biblical text. Fortunately we are living now in a time when a major shift going on in biblical studies encourages those of us who preach in this process of energetically attending to the text. I am talking about the move toward literary and rhetorical criticism. This is, of course, a complex development, but let me risk some oversimplification by observing that one of the results of the literary move in biblical studies is to empower those of us who preach to trust our own interaction with biblical texts.

You see, if the meaning of a biblical text is only located behind the text in history, then only historians can get at it, and those with the sharpest historical tools can get at it best. So we preachers sit down at the desk with a passage from the Gospel of John and several commentaries written by highly-trained historians, and there we are, in a seminar with Raymond Brown, C.H. Dodd, and Rudolf Bultmann. No wonder we do not say much. The experts tell us what the text used to mean and then, when they are safely out of the room, we muddle around trying to figure out how to say what it now means, what it used to mean, thus and so.

The claim now is that a text's meaning is not confined to what it used to mean. Texts are rhetorical events and the meanings of a biblical text are also located in front of the text creating ever new meanings with each new encounter. This does not imply that we have a license to do eisegesis, an invitation to treat texts as Rorschach blots, or permission to get rid of Drs. Brown, Dodd, and Bultmann. We do not get rid of the experts; we just change their job description. They are no longer there to tell us what this text means, because they cannot. What a text means is a product of the interaction between the text itself and a particular situation, and we are the ones—the only ones—in a position to discover what this text wants to say to these people on this day. The job of the experts is to clear the landscape of false assumptions, to filter out the noise of misunderstanding, to establish the text to which we are to listen. The experts can show us the rules, and they can tell us when we have stepped out of bounds, but we have to play the game.

Interpreting a text for preaching is something like exploring a cave. We go exploring into the cavern of the text, searching not just for ourselves, but also for the people who have sent us there on their behalf and to whom we will preach. We do not yet know exactly what we are looking for, but we will know it when we find it. We shine our flashlight around in the darkness, and we see there the evidence that we are not the first to explore this cave. Explorer Irenaeus has carved an inscription on the wall. Explorer Von Rad has left a note telling us that this passageway leads to a dead end. Explorer Guttierez has left a manual explaining how a particular rock formation came to be. Thus we keep looking until, there it is; that is what we have been looking for. It may be a breathtaking waterfall or a wall shimmering with jewels, but we know this is what we have been seeking because it grips us and makes a claim on us, and we know that it will do the same for all we are there representing. We now retrace our steps to the mouth of the cave, check our watches and find that it is Sunday morning, and there is our congregation waiting on us.

With dirt still on our faces and our flashlights in hand, we say to them, "Have I got something to show you! Come with me."

Another advantage in the rhetorical approach to scriptural interpretation is that it sensitizes us to the many different ways of speaking that are found in the Bible. The faith does not get proclaimed with only one inflection, but in a chorus of dialects. Part of what I mean by this is that biblical texts are not only concerned with *saying* things; they are also interested in *doing* things, and that means they say what they say in different ways. A parable and an epistle may seem to say roughly the same thing, but the fact that one is a parable and one is an epistle means that they are doing different things in the consciousness of readers and hearers. Preaching that is faithful to a biblical text sometimes will seek not only to say what the text says but also to do what the text does.

Let me give an example of what I am talking about, and in order not to make this too easy on myself, let me pick a hard case, namely proverbs. How long has it been since you preached on a proverb?

Suppose we decide to try that; the first thing we have to know is what a proverb is trying to do. Some people think that biblical proverbs are like the sayings found in *Poor Richard's Almanac.* They are little bits of banal advice on how to be wise and successful intended for the consumption of people who are neither; "A penny saved is a penny earned," and so on. That is not exactly what biblical proverbs are. Proverbs are the expression of the wisdom tradition in our faith, and that tradition comes from the interaction between people of faithful vision and discernment, the sages, and raw human experience.

The wisdom tradition acknowledges that appearances are deceiving, that what looks at first glance like a satisfying and rewarding life can actually be foolish and impoverished self-deception. So, the sage looks out with the eyes of faith at the chaos of life and tries to sift what is authentic and wise in human behavior from what is destructive and then put that into a saying which can be remembered and used by others as a lens to see life more clearly. The first question of the sage is not, "How are people supposed to behave?" but rather, "What's going on around here?" What is happening in life when you view it with eyes of faith? "The fear of the Lord is the beginning of wisdom."

That is why biblical proverbs often contradict themselves. One saying in the book of Proverbs says, "Don't answer a fool according to his folly, lest you be like him." The very next verse, however, says, "Answer a fool according to his folly, lest he be wise in his own eyes" (Prov. 26:5). "He who is not with me is against me," Jesus says in one place (Matt. 12:30). "He that is not against you is for you," he says in another (Luke 9:50). Proverbs sometimes contradict themselves because they are not intended to be universal truths which float above time and circumstance, little quips we cross-stitch and hang on the kitchen wall; "If life gives you lemons, make lemonade." Proverbs grow out of certain kinds of real experience, and they cannot be separated from those experiences. They make sense only in relationship to those types of experience.

With this fact in mind, what do proverbs do? They provide memorable and portable sayings which people can carry into certain human experiences and use to see those experiences more deeply for what they are and know how to live faithfully in them. If that is true, then I believe we ought to be doing more proverbial preaching. It is a neglected voice in biblical preaching.

In his book *The Moral Context of Pastoral Care*, Don Browning speaks about the development of pastoral counseling methods in contemporary ministry.[3] He says that there was a time when people in trouble would come to the pastor's office because, even though it was clear out there in the world how they were supposed to be living, they were unable to meet those demands. The pastor's task was to suspend temporarily the moral obligations, to say to the person, "Look, in here there is no right and wrong; there is only total acceptance," and then when the person had put things back together a bit, he or she could be sent back out into the world of moral demands.

Now, says Browning, the situation has changed. It is no longer clear out in the world what are the moral obligations, and people are increasingly coming to their pastors seeking not the suspension of moral categories, but wisdom: "How should I live?"

When Elie Wiesel accepted his Nobel Peace Prize last year he gave a speech which sounded like a sermon, and a proverbial sermon at that. "No one is more capable of gratitude," he said, "than one who has emerged from death's kingdom. Every moment is a gift of grace." He also said, "As long as one child is hungry, our lives are filled with . . . shame."⁴ Those are proverbs.

I can imagine a sermon preached in the proverbial voice which would use the wisdom saying as a refrain, and move back and forth between this saying and the human experience in which it is true.

One of my favorite hobbies is making fun of the self-help paperbacks, which sell by the carload, but it occurred to me not long ago in the middle of my mirth that people are actually living their lives out of these things, their real and only lives. So I did what I had never done before. I bought one and read it. Sure enough, it was full of foolishness masquerading as wisdom, but what struck me more than anything else was the style in which it was written. It was proverbs—bad proverbs—but it was proverbs. People live their lives out of proverbs. My faith tells me that the biblical proverb, "Treasures gained by wickedness do not profit, but justice delivers from death," is a wiser proverb than "Look out for Number One," but if I think so, then I believe I'd better learn how to preach occasionally in a proverbial voice.

If paying attention to the many voices in Scripture is one way to find our voice in preaching, paying attention to our theological tradition is another. I was complaining to one of our systematic theologians the other day that one of the most discouraging things to me as a teacher is to hear a seminary senior preach a sermon which voices the very same theology that he or she brought to seminary, untouched by the experience of theological education. They are reading the best theology from all around the world and from all periods in the history of the church, and they are making "A's" on theology papers, but in too many cases this knowledge never makes it to the pulpit. In the classroom they can dissect the Council of Nicaea, but in the pulpit what often comes out is that Jesus was a friendly, divine phantom who died on the cross so that we can have "quiet time."

Lest I come across as too hard on the students, let me hasten to say that I know that much of the problem is in the way we do theology in the academy. We do theology—well, academically—and that creates the impression that there are two kinds of theology. One is a kind of mental chess game in which you move pieces around on some board, and the other is the kind you live your real life out of, and these two types do not intersect.

William Muehl tells about the student who attended Yale Divinity School a number of years ago who became infatuated with the theology of Karl Barth. In the name of Barth, this student "harangued seminars, gave chapel talks which were mini-lectures on Barth," and, when he preached, he gave congregations forty-minute expositions of the latest volume in the *Dogmatics*.

Ten years after this student finally graduated to take Barth to the world, he returned to Yale for an alumni event, and Muehl was surprised to see that his former student wore in his lapel a button "which proclaimed him a fan of one of America's most popular positive-thinking media preachers," a preacher whose ideas were about as far away from Barth's as one could get. When Muehl asked him about this, he looked embarrassed, and then finally confessed, "I lost three churches before I learned what people want from the pulpit. So now I give it to them."[5]

What we need to learn is that there are more than two options. We are not in the position of either giving them Barth or giving them what we think they want. There is a third option. As Muehl goes on to say:

The struggle of the preacher to communicate what was of value in the seminary experience can and ought to be an opportunity for *doing theology* in the most creative way. . . . As the pastor grapples with the relevance of classroom lectures to a complex of living room and board room problems, he or she is going through a professional version of what the laity is being called to do in the context of its own responsibilities and challenges in home and office. . . . (The laity) have, for the most part, some fragmentary religious commitments that are related to one another and to some degree integrated in the give-and-take of . . . "the real world." . . . (F)or them the flow of influence between theology and practice is a two-way street.[6]

The third option is to place formal theology right out there in the middle of the two-way street, to let it interact with the real experiences of our people, to break down the walls between classroom theology and street theology. Now, that is, we must admit, a difficult skill, and in order to explore an example of what this might look like, let us take on what is surely the test par excellence of theological preaching: the Easter sermon and the question of the resurrection.

I heard the question of the resurrection being discussed in the streets a couple of months ago, by the way. When I say "the streets," in this case I mean the *New York Times,* which is one of the crossroads of our culture, and there they were talking about Jesus and the resurrection. That is fitting, I suppose, because part of the theological claim of the resurrection is that you can never tell just where Jesus is going to show up. Sure enough, there he was in the pages of the *New York Times Book Review.* There amid talk of the latest psychobiography of Flaubert, the most recent feminist dissection of social hierarchies, and yet another analysis of the decline and fall of modern marriage, was Jesus of Nazareth, looking as out-of-place as Saint Francis at a $500-a-plate political fund-raiser.

What prompted Jesus' appearance in the *Times* was an essay called "Jesus Among the Historians," written by the eminent Roman Catholic biblical scholar John P. Meier.[7] It was ostensibly a review of E.P. Sanders' book, *Jesus and Judaism,* but the real focus of interest was neither Sanders nor his book, but his subject: Jesus.

Since the Book Review section of the Sunday *Times* is designed to be read by people who are killing time between Sunday brunch and "Masterpiece Theater," there is obviously some opportunity for subtle evangelism there, and Meier was rising nicely to the task. He was respectful of the fact that he was on the American equivalent of Mars Hill talking to moderns and skeptics. He was careful to maintain the precise methods and to speak in the measured prose of the careful historian, saying no more than the evidence would merit. However, the man was scoring some preaching points, no question about it.

Before he got to the resurrection, Meier talked about the New Testament record of Jesus' miracles. He cleared his academic throat by observing that "how one explains the phenomena [of miracle working in ancient and modern religion] varies with both the subject studied and the observer commenting." Cautious enough, but then, without catching his breath, he announced in the very next sentence:

> In the case of Jesus, all that need be noted is that ancient Christian, Jewish and pagan sources all agreed that Jesus did extraordinary things not easily explained by human means.[8]

All that need be noted—indeed. If I read him correctly, what Meier was saying in his understated way, was that if you had been there in the synagogue at Capernaum the day the man with the withered hand got called up to the front, glanced around nervously at the stony congregation, stretched out his hand, and suddenly found that for the first time in his life he could extend his arms to embrace a friend without shame, you may have gasped with amazement, sung a psalm in gratitude, or maybe even have rushed off to Herod's office to see if the government could put an end to such interruptions of the liturgy. But, be you Jewish, Christian, or pagan, you would not have tottered casually off to brunch.

As for Jesus the teacher, Meier notes accurately, if somewhat obviously, that many of Jesus' pronouncements—on mercy without measure, on love without limits, on forgiveness without boundaries—seem to contemporary people to be noble ideals, but "simply unattainable." Fair enough, but Meier does not leave it there. He looks the reader straight in the eye, pauses, then calmly states:

> To Jesus, they were possible, but only for those who had experienced through Him God's incredible love changing their lives. Radical demand flowed from radical grace. If religion was grace, then ethics was gratitude.[9]

After that, can we really move casually on to the review of the newest book on Marilyn Monroe? But Meier is not finished. He patiently walks his readers through the synoptic problem, the thorny matter of Jesus' self-consciousness, the complex question of what can be firmly known about Jesus versus that which was the invention of pious imagination, always obeying the constraints of historical evidence, but straining here and there at the tether to give witness to the challenges of this remarkable human being from Nazareth. "The kingdom was somehow already present in His person and ministry," reports Meier, "and on the last day He would be the criterion by which people would be judged."

And then—and then—Meier finally arrives at the resurrection. Here his pen falters, and his decisive voice grows curiously quiet. "Since the Jesus of history," he finally states, "is by definition open to empirical investigation by any and all observers, the resurrection of Jesus, of its very nature, lies outside the scope of this essay. This does not mean that the resurrection is not real, but simply that it is not an ordinary event of our time and space, verifiable in principle by believer and nonbeliever alike."[10]

There you have it. The trail of the historical Jesus, we are told, is a fascinating path full of wonders and rich insights, available to be traveled by all, but it leads inexorably to a precipice. All history can say is that Jesus died on a Roman cross, and that, as Meier reminds us, "starting in the early 30's of the first century, people who had known Jesus during His earthly life and who had deserted Him out of fear did a remarkable about-face after His disgraceful death and affirmed that

Jesus had risen and appeared to them."[11] On one side of the precipice, then, is only a record of capital punishment and a few scraps of information about the beginnings of a religious movement. On the other side is whatever it was that turned Peter from a coward to a martyr, but history alone cannot take us across the gap.

And there stands the preacher on Easter, straddling the gap, one foot firmly placed on the side of history and tangibility where people believe only what they can see and touch, the other foot shakily reaching toward, if not firmly placed upon, the mysterious ground of resurrection faith. What to say—what to say?

No wonder the sermonic pen falters and the homiletical voice becomes mute in the days before Easter. No wonder that Easter, the one day in the year that most lay people naively assume must be their minister's very favorite day—what with the crowded sanctuary and the choir in full voice—is, in fact, held in secret terror by many of the clergy. On every other Sunday the clever preacher can, if inclined, parry and thrust with a few Churchill quotes, tell a couple of cute animal stories, and usually get away with pretending that the Christian faith is, after all, not really so unreasonable. But on Easter, the preacher must straddle the awe-ful gap, must stand up there before people who are wearing wrist watches, carrying credit cards, and wondering if their just-filed income tax returns are going to be audited, and tell them that it is the truth—the truth above all truths—that Jesus Christ was raised from the dead. "Now when they heard of the resurrection of the dead, some mocked" (Acts 17:32a).

No wonder such excitement surrounded the famous Shroud of Turin. It seemed to be a piece of concrete evidence graciously tossed from the far side of the chasm to the near. If it were what some claim it is, the very burial cloth of Jesus with an image implanted by a powerful burst of energy, then it is no less than a photograph of the resurrection able to be studied with electron microscopes and hung in a museum for all to see, a sign from heaven.

Those who truly know the way of the gospel know there is no such sign, however, no piece of irrefutable evidence we can take out into that two-way street, no steel bridge from here to the resurrection. We have only word of mouth, generation to generation. We have only the voice of the preacher, blown by the wind of the Spirit, to span the gap. "The best Easter sermon that I have heard or read in the United States during the past ten years," Markus Barth once wrote,

> was an honest expression of the preacher's complete bafflement by the Resurrection stories. . . . It was a confession of lack of understanding; it revealed want of appropriation, and failure of communication. It was a cry for help and enlightenment: Here it is said that Thou art risen. But, where are you now? How can we believe? Help our unbelief!—This preacher did more than take the Resurrection seriously. He could not stand up to it; like John of Patmos he just fell down.[12]

All genuine gospel preaching on Easter is first a falling down before the mystery of the resurrection, but it is not only that. It is also a getting back up again to say what we can say. A good place to begin considering just what that might be is in the ancient record of another preacher's struggle with what to say about the resurrection. I am talking about Paul's famous and convoluted statement in 1 Corinthians 15.

At one time I viewed 1 Corinthians 15 as perhaps the most disappointing of all New Testament passages, because it apparently delivered so little after promising so much. Earlier in my youth some well-meaning preacher had fixed it in my mind that this text was a product of the crystalline logic of Paul's formidable theological mind, and that, properly understood, it constituted an irrefutable proof of the resurrection. When I became old enough to examine such claims for myself, however, I never could get the logic of the passage to work. At the time I had never heard the phrase "circular argument," but if I had, I would certainly have applied it to this passage.

"I have preached to you," Paul's argument seemed to go, "that Christ is raised from the dead. Now if I have preached that to you, how can some of you say that there is no resurrection of the dead?" (This was, to my mind, a promising start, with exactly the correct question raised. I hastened on to see how Paul answered his own query.) "Now if there is no resurrection of the dead, then Christ has not been raised, and that would mean that I didn't tell the truth in my preaching and your faith is in vain. But I *did* tell the truth in my preaching and, in fact, I'm going to preach that truth to you again, 'Christ has been raised from the dead.'" (To my mind, this was no example of crystalline logic; this was a merry-go-round, and I wanted off.)

The text was a disappointment to me then because it seemed to promise proof, but to deliver only more preaching. It seems to me now, though, that I seriously misunderstood the way the logic of the passage actually works and, therefore, missed a crucial insight about the resurrection.

The text *is* an argument of the "if this, then this" variety; I was right about that. I was also correct about the notion that such arguments cannot hang in mid-air. They must touch ground *somewhere* by appealing to *something* that even the skeptic must admit is true. Suppose I am trying to convince you that a mutual friend, Bob Smith, was not in church last Sunday. It will not do simply to jump up and down and insist that he was absent. I need an *argument,* so I construct the following: "If Bob was in Hong Kong last Sunday, then he was not in our town, and, if he was not in our town, he, therefore could not have been present in church." So far, so good; the logic chain makes sense. Now, for this to work, I need some proof for the *first* item in the chain. I need a photograph, an affidavit, a telephone call record, or something of the sort which will verify to you and anyone else who is interested that Bob was, indeed, in Hong Kong last Sunday. If I can produce the evidence, then you will have to bow to the logic of my argument. The chain moves deductively from what we definitely know to that which can be logically inferred from that knowledge.

What I failed to see was that not all "if this, then this" arguments move that way. Sometimes the argument is not

grounded at the *beginning* of the chain, but at the *end*.
Sometimes such arguments do not move *from* what we definitely know, but *toward* it. Suppose we try my argument that
way. "If Bob was in Hong Kong last Sunday," I say, "then he
was not in our town, and, if he was not in our town, he therefore could not have been present in church."

Then suppose *you* say, "But he *was* in church last Sunday.
He sang in the choir. I saw him. I heard him. You saw him,
too." Ah, now, because you know and trust your own experience, the logic of the argument begins to run the other way.
"We *experienced* Bob present in church. Therefore, he was *not*
out of town; he was *not* in Hong Kong." In this case, what we
definitely know comes at the *end* of the chain and ripples back
toward the beginning.

And that is precisely how the logic of the Pauline argument runs:

> If there is no resurrection of the dead . . .
>   . . . then Christ has not been raised
> And if Christ has not been raised . . .
>   . . . then our preaching was a lie
> And if our preaching was a lie . . .
>   . . . then your faith is futile

At this point, and this is the key, the Corinthians would
shout in unison, "But, our faith is *not* futile." Even the badly
divided Corinthians—squabbling about the Lord's Supper,
pointing fingers at each other about eating meat fresh off
some pagan altar, crossing swords over tongue-speaking,
splitting hairs over church leadership—*even* the Corinthians
would agree about this one thing: their faith was *not* in vain.
They had, if nothing else, a lively faith, a dynamic sense of
the experience of the risen Christ in their midst. Their zeal
threatened on occasion to burn down the church, but they did
have zeal. "In every way you were enriched in God," writes
Paul, "with all speech and all knowledge, even as the testimony to Christ was confirmed among you." In other words,
amazing, troubling, mysterious, and energizing things were
happening at Corinth. If you worshiped at Corinth on Sunday,

you might go away filled with the Holy Spirit or you might go away mad, but you would not just go away, tottering off casually to brunch.

So Paul's argument does not work from the beginning to the end, but from the end back toward the beginning. Because the one thing the Corinthians were sure of was the electric quality of their faith through the charismatic presence of Christ, they would exclaim "No!" to the assertion, "Your faith is in vain." This "no," really this affirmation of their faith experience, would then flow back through the entire chain of the argument, changing the value of the signs from minus to plus, thus: our faith *is* alive, we know that. Therefore Paul's preaching that brought us to this faith *was* the truth, and Christ *is* raised indeed, and, therefore, we *can* affirm with conviction the resurrection from the dead.

The point here is exceedingly important for Easter preaching. If on Easter we try to find our way from our age to the resurrection of Jesus, we will only find that there is no way to get there from here. Meier is right, the resurrection "is not an ordinary event of our time and space," and, as such, it is not only outside the scope of Meier's essay, it is also outside of our grasp. All we will find are an empty tomb, perhaps an abandoned shroud, and the sociological data of an eccentric new religious movement.

Easter preaching does not begin, then, with people's general inquisitiveness about what really happened that Sunday morning long ago, trying to coax that curiosity gradually into a reasonable recitation of the Apostles' Creed. Nor does it begin by explaining the mechanics of the doctrine of the resurrection and then beckoning people to muster up what it takes to believe in it. Easter preaching begins with the vision that the Risen Christ is present and at work in the world and that people everywhere experience the power of this living Christ and feel Christ's claim upon their lives.

In short, Easter preaching begins with people's experience—not just their ordinary experience, but with their experience, clearly felt or vaguely sensed, of the Risen Christ. As

Hans-Rudolf Muller-Schwefe once put it, "'Did not our hearts burn?' (Luke 24:32) is the theme of Easter."[13] Most of those who show up in the pews on Easter are there because, to some degree and in some way, they have heard Christ calling to them, and they have come searching for the words which will enable them to say, "Our faith is not in vain." The gift of being able to speak those words is what the Easter sermon is all about.

Now it may sound as though, by pointing to experience as the starting point for Easter preaching, I am abandoning what I set out to do, namely, listening to the theological tradition, and instead issuing a license to push aside the books of systematic theology, to abandon gleefully all closely-reasoned analyses of the doctrine of the resurrection in favor of a more exciting romp through people's religious experience. That is not at all what I have in mind. In fact, the understanding of Easter preaching I am describing will send us quickly and deeply into every responsible theological treatment of the resurrection we can get our hands on. But we will go there not in order to find out what people are supposed to believe about the resurrection so that we can explain it to them. We will, rather, go to theology because it will teach *us* where to look and how to look for the power of the Risen Christ in human experience.

One of the first such lessons theology has to teach us is that the resurrection of Christ serves to validate the ministry of Jesus. As Carl Braaten puts it: the risen Christ who is present with us now "is identical with the one who was—the Jesus of history. The risen Lord is continuous with the crucified Jesus."[14]

This seemingly innocuous theological statement is actually quite important for Easter preaching. There are plenty of people whose Christian faith and practice consists of various attempts to follow Jesus as the model for their own living. As one pastor recently told me, "If I make a strong theological and ethical case for the liberation of the oppressed, my people shrug and yawn, but if I tell them the stories of Jesus caring for the poor and hungry, they ask, 'What can we do to help?'" It is easy, of course, to take shots at a simplistic "What would Jesus do?"

approach, but finally to look down upon such efforts is to miss the point of Easter. The resurrection validates the earthly ministry of Jesus as the way of God, and far from condescending to attempts by Christian people to live like Jesus lived, the resurrection lifts such energies to the highest power.

I attend a church that prides itself on its ability to appeal to the educated sensibilities of the residents of our university town. Not long ago I found myself at a "covered-dish" dinner at this church, seated next to a man whom I had seen around the church, but never met. We introduced ourselves to each other, and he asked me how long I had been attending that church. "Only about two years," I replied. "We're fairly new in town. How about you?"

"I've been in this church for years," he answered. "In fact, I'm the only nonintellectual left in this congregation."

"You're kidding," I ventured with a smile.

"No I'm not. I haven't understood a sermon that's been preached here in twenty-five years."

I weakly suggested that he must surely be exaggerating, but he was clearly in the middle of a point.

"But I'll tell you one thing," he went on. "I'd *never* leave this church."

When I asked why, he told me that for several years, every Monday night, he and a few others had been taking the church van to a nearby prison for youthful offenders. "Sometimes we play ball with the kids," he said. "Sometimes we have a little Bible study. Most of all we just get to know them as people. I started doing this because Christians are *supposed* to do things like that, but now I find that I get a lot from it myself." He paused for a moment, then continued, "I have found that you can't prove the promises of God in advance, but if you live them, you find they're true, every one."

What can we say in an Easter sermon to that man who is visiting a prison because Jesus said to do so and who "hasn't understood a sermon in twenty-five years"? He probably would not warm up to, "The resurrection validates the ministry of Jesus," but how about, "Your faith is not in vain"?

Another insight theology gives us is that the resurrection is God's promise of the future intended for humanity. As Hendrikus Berkhof expressed it, "(Jesus') glorification is the ground of our coming glorification. As the first and only one he is at the same time the firstfruits."[15] The writer of 1 John puts it another way, "It does not yet appear what we shall be, but we know that when he appears we shall be like him" (1 John 3:2).

The implications of this are, of course, many, but one thing we can surely say is that the resurrection opens the way for all human rebellions against determinism and hopelessness. The resurrection reveals that the phrase "history repeats itself" is too nearsighted to serve as a creed. If history endlessly repeated itself, dead people would remain dead, and the women who came to the tomb would have found there a decaying body in need of some fragrant spices. Instead they found that God's tomorrow is not confined to yesterday's tragedy, but is open, free, moving, and alive.

Some people live toward this future, even if they do not know how to name it. Some people say, "The poor are always with us," and, with a shrug of the shoulder, walk away to make the next payment on the Mercedes. Other people, however, sacrificially share their possessions from warm and generous hearts. Why? Some people say "There will be wars and rumors of wars," and just hope that when the time comes we have more firepower than the other guys. Other people pray for peace, work for peace, and live as makers of peace. Why? Some people say, "Once a jerk, always a jerk," and let many suns go down on their anger. Other people forgive and forgive, seven times seventy. Why?

The only sensible answer lies in the fundamental assumptions we make about the future. If tomorrow is to be just like today, only more so, then only a fool would forgive, pray, love, and sacrifice. To be sure, some prudent planning might be in order so that we can draw the best available hand from the present deck, but we already know what is in the cards.

But if the tomb could not remain sealed, if suffering and death do not have the last word, if God's future for us is more than an infinite extension of yesterday, then we can hope for more than a reshuffling of the same old cards. A radically new game has been promised.

A theory currently in vogue among some physicists holds that the movement of time is connected to the expansion of the universe. As long as the universe is expanding, goes the theory, time flows along from past to future. If for any reason, though, the universe should begin to contract, time itself would reverse. People, if they were able to survive such a shift, would journey from age to youth, from the grave to the cradle, and they would "remember what is to happen tomorrow." Some of these theorists have even suggested that our universe has a mirror-imaged twin, which is now operating from future to past. In this universe, composed of antimatter, time runs backward.[16]

If such an alternative universe exists, I do not care to live there. I find utterly terrifying the thought of a life in which every detail of the future is predetermined. However, the sad truth is that, existentially, many people already live in that universe. The tragic facts of human life are already fixed, and all that remains is the joyless living out of them.

. In Flannery O'Connor's *A Good Man is Hard to Find,* a notorious outlaw called the Misfit terrorizes, and finally murders, a family who have had an auto accident on a lonely rural road. One member of the family, the grandmother, as she fears for her life calls out, "Jesus, Jesus." The Misfit responds,

"Jesus was the only One that ever raised the dead. . . . and He shouldn't have done it. He thrown everything off balance. If He did what He said, then it's nothing for you to do but throw away everything and follow Him, and if He didn't, then it's nothing for you to do but enjoy the few minutes you got left the best way you can—by killing somebody or burning down his house or doing some other meanness to him. No pleasure but meanness." (From A GOOD MAN IS HARD TO FIND AND OTHER STORIES, copyright 1953 by Flannery O'Connor; renewed 1981 by Mrs. Regina O'Connor. Reprinted by permission of Harcourt Brace Jovanovich, Inc.)

In his own grisly way, the Misfit spoke the truth. Either

the mean facts of life are already set, and there is nothing to do but grab what we can in the few ticks of the clock we have left, or "He did what He said." If the latter is true, then everything is indeed off balance. Life is asymmetrical; the sands of the past do not pour into an identical sealed chamber, only to have the hour-glass turned over to repeat the same closed sequence. The tragic past flows instead toward redemption.

It is perhaps the most remarkable of all human phenomena that there are people who insist on living their lives as if the dice are not, in fact, loaded. I am talking, of course, about the Martin Luthers and the Martin Luther Kings, but I am also speaking of the people who will be out there in the pews on Easter morning. They are having children in uncertain times and serving up soup to the homeless and giving their money to the Cancer Society and praying for justice for poor people in countries whose names they can hardly pronounce and writing letters to people in jail and trying to stammer out why they believe in God to people seated next to them on airplanes and being hospitable to strangers and in countless other ways betting their lives on a future more gracious and redemptive than they or anyone else can possibly create by mere human effort.

I know that faithlessness is out there, too. I know that there are plenty of church-goers whose creed is progress, whose savior is technology, and whose sacrament is cash. But that is not the whole story. In a world where Christ is not one idea among many, but a living presence, that *cannot be* the whole story.

I know a couple who have every reason to let their lives slip safely into some predictable groove. They are politically conservative, socially cautious by nature. They are retired. Their income is fixed, but comfortable. Their children are successfully raised and gone. They have every reason to pat themselves on the back for a job well done, turn on the television, and relax. Through a program in their church, however, they began to write to a man in prison. It began slowly—a chatty letter every now and then, a card and a box of cookies on his birthday. Then one visit and another. Then the man is paroled, out, free, a human being to be faced and dealt with. On Christmas Day, when most retired folks with stocks and bonds were carving the turkey and figuring out how to wangle the best tax advantage before year's end, this couple gave thanks and broke bread in their home with their newly-released friend in Christ. "I think he was convicted of armed robbery, we're not sure," one of them told me. "Anyway, it was good to have him in our home." What do you say to these people on Easter? How about, "Your faith is not in vain"?

Theology teaches us to look for evidence of the living Christ in yet another place in people's experience. It sounds like a cliche to say it, but we must not let that dissuade us. Despite the fact that these words on the lips of some can be trite, it is nontheless true that the power of the Risen Christ can be seen in all efforts to love others, especially the unlovely.

It is one of the ironies of contemporary church life that the fundamental claim of the gospel to love those whom the world rejects has become associated in the minds of many with theological parties, and, in particular, with the bureaucracies of the big denominations. The fact that cumbersome, ideologically-centered phrases, like "marginalized persons" and "liberation of the oppressed," are fighting words to many people and groups in the church today should not be allowed to obscure the greater truths that the Risen Christ indeed calls us to love those who, on ordinary grounds, would be our castoffs and even our enemies, and furthermore that there are people, many of whom do not know the bureaucratic jargon, who strive to exhibit just that kind of love.

Where can this kind of love be seen? It can be seen in those families who choose to adopt the "unadoptable" child. It can be seen in those who tirelessly circulate petitions aimed at warming the political hearts of city halls grown cold to the homeless in the streets. It can be seen in those who sit caringly beside beds in nursing homes. It can be seen in those who give up cherished leisure time to refurbish houses for refugees. It can be seen wherever people show active and loving concern for any victim.

But it would be a half-truth to speak only of love for victims.

For some, what appears to be love for victims is actually the energy produced by hatred for the victimizers. Resurrection love is more radical than that. The One whom God raised was Jesus, who ate and drank with prostitutes and tax collectors, with victims and victimizers. As Moltmann put it:

> The message [the gospel] brings into the world says that in fact the executioners will not finally triumph over their victims. It also says that in the end the victims will not triumph over their executioners. The one will triumph who first died for the victims and then also for the executioners, and in so doing revealed a new righteousness which breaks through the vicious circles of hate and vengeance.[17]

It must be said, of course, that love for an oppressor is not always perceived by the oppressor as love, since sometimes this love comes in the form of protest and confrontation. But it must also not be forgotten that it is possible for confrontation to be born of love rather than of hatred.

Early in my ministry I found myself embroiled in a rather nasty theological fight at the denominational level. The issue of the conflict has long since faded, but not so the memories of the bitterness which existed between the two sides. As is often the case in such disputes, the opposing groups were not just debating parties; they were feared enemies, each side persuaded that the other sought to undermine the faithfulness of the church.

During one of the most acrimonious seasons of this struggle, we learned that our four-week-old daughter would have to be hospitalized for surgery. We had been assured that the surgery would be successful (and, as it turned out, it was), but we were new parents; she was our only child, and it was a dark and frightening time. The day before the surgery, I received a telephone call from one of the leaders of the other group in the theological dispute. I groaned to myself. Not now, I beg you. Not now.

Then the voice on the other end of the line spoke an unexpected message. "I heard the news about your daughter," he said. "I want you to know that she, and you, are in my prayers." Something about the hesitancy in his voice let me know that this was not the expression of pious sentiment. Something about the character of Christian love had struggled free from the grip of enmity and found expression through him.

"Thank you. That means more than I can say." That is what I said to him. I wish I had added, "Your faith is not in vain."

Seeking to live the life that Jesus lived. Hoping toward a redemptive future we cannot fully see. Loving those we would not ordinarily love. These are but a few of the many truths to be discovered by the Easter preacher in the doctrine of the resurrection, the many ways in which the power of the Risen Christ can be seen and felt in human experience. The ways are so many, I suppose, that they can not be numbered, because, when all is said and done, the resurrection is the claim that you can never tell just where Jesus is going to show up. And that is the best news our voices are privileged to speak.

Chapter 3

The Ears of Preaching

The first sermon I ever preached to a real live congregation was based on 1 Chronicles 17. That is the story, you may remember, about the time King David realized that he, the king, lived in a magnificent cedar house, but that the Ark of the Covenant was housed under a mere tent. On the theory that God should not live in canvas while the king lived in cedar, David set out to build God a fancy house of cedar, too. Nathan the prophet at first thought this was a fine idea, but God spoke to him in the night and changed his mind. "Go tell David," said the voice of the Lord, "you shall not build me a house, for I haven't dwelt in a house since the day I began leading Israel, but I've gone from tent to tent and dwelling to dwelling."

Well, I was a seminary student; I thought that was a pretty good text with a fairly clear message, so I took a sermon on it into my first series of encounters with genuine congregations. One of these was a small flock of rural Georgians in one of those forsaken little churches in some presbytery's intensive care ward. Their only possessions were a cemetery, a decaying building, and a silver communion set. They had no program, no youth, no leadership, no prospect for growth, and no minister in the last fifteen years, just week after week of seminary students trying out our wings.

I stood up to preach, and I am sure I looked eager and a bit nervous. They, on the other hand, looked as though they were about to have root canal work. And I preached. "God does not live in buildings made with hands," I said, pointing my finger at the soiled walls of their very own sanctuary. "God despises buildings and monuments," my gesture now sweeping unconsciously in the direction of the cemetery. "God is out there in the world, moving with the wind, tent to tent and dwelling to dwelling, calling us to follow in a life of never-ending change." It may have been my imagination, but as I preached, I thought you could have heard a pin drop.

At the door—nothing. Just one limp handshake after another, an occasional "nice to have you," and basically that look which rural Georgians reserve for seminary students from Atlanta. I was discouraged, but then—hope. The last man out of the door startled me by pumping my hand vigorously. "Best sermon I have ever heard!" he practically shouted. "And I want you to know that I agree with you one hundred percent!"

"You do?" I stammered.

"Yes I do. You're right as you can be, son. We do need more tent revivals!"

What an experience. Those who heard me did not approve, and the one who approved did not hear me. From the earliest days of my preaching ministry, then, I have been intrigued by the question of what it is that people actually hear in sermons. How much control does the preacher have, should the preacher try to take, in what people hear in sermons?

Back in the 1960s a number of studies were done on congregations trying to determine what they had actually heard in sermons, as opposed to what their preachers had been trying to say. Most of these studies involved people filling out questionnaires right after worship about the sermons they had just heard, and many of these surveys were conducted by people who were convinced that preaching was a monumental waste of ministerial time and energy. Sure enough, they found what they were looking for and gleefully reported the results. Sermons, they announced, are the "chicken chow mein" of ministry. Many listeners, they found, could not remember what the sermon was about fifteen minutes after hearing it, and even those who thought they could remember routinely described the sermon in terms vastly different from the actual message delivered by the preacher.

Incidentally, I have found in my own experience that this phenomenon is not confined to the laity. Occasionally in preaching workshops, because I am looking for a live and current example, I will ask one of the ministers participating to describe the sermon she or he preached last Sunday. Eventually it comes, but usually not until after a moment of panic and some embarrassed scratching of the head trying to recall what, in fact, last week's sermon was about.

The message of all these studies was clear: preaching is a notoriously unreliable form of communication. If any ministers insist on continuing to do it, they ought to do so free from the illusion that what is heard will bear any resemblance to what they have said.

One of these critics, Clyde Reid, suggested that lay people come to sermons with their ears covered. "If this covered ears theory of preaching has validity," he announced,

> it would help to explain why many people continue to attend church even when they are not listening to the minister's message. They may be experiencing an unconscious sense of being punished and having atoned for their misdeeds simply by going through the motions of sitting quietly and appearing to listen. As a result, they go away feeling whole and clean or forgiven. The minister, for his part, could go away feeling satisfied that he has "straightened his children out," which makes him feel important and fulfilled. The covered ears theory may also help us understand why only one person in five can tell us the main idea in the minister's sermon following the service.[1]

Reid was clearly pushing a few statistical scraps to their most cynical conclusion, but these disturbing studies obviously have some basis in fact, and they need to be taken seriously. Part of what they spotted as a problem for preaching resides in the fact that preaching is often poorly done. People cannot remember, or they misremember, what was said because what was said was illogical, incoherent, or not worth remembering in the first place. I want to devote most of the space in this chapter to addressing this kind of problem in sermons.

Before we do that, however, I think it is important to say that some of these studies seem damning not because preaching is an untrustworthy form of communication, but because the researchers failed to understand what kind of communication preaching actually is in the first place. I want to explore that for a moment, not because I think we should necessarily be interested in twenty-year-old studies of preaching, but because I think some of the assumptions the researchers made still lurk in the minds of those of us who preach.

To begin with, many of us have a false picture in our heads of what can and should happen in human communication. Much of the research, in fact, was based on a model borrowed from the world of electronic communication. You have probably seen it before; many homiletics texts have used it. It goes:

SOURCE—MESSAGE—CHANNEL—RECEIVER

The idea is that when communication occurs, some source sends data, encoded in the form of a message, through a particular channel to a receiver. You can see why homileticians jumped eagerly on this model. All we have to do is rename the components of the model. The source? Why, that is the preacher, of course. The message? The content of the preaching encoded in words both theological and otherwise. The channel? It could have been the newsletter or a pastoral visit. These are both channels available to the minister for sending messages, but in our case it is the Sunday sermon spoken in the liturgical context. The receiver? The hearers. Simple enough. The model becomes a preaching model.

The problem here is that if we trace the ancestry of this model all the way back to its origin, we will find that its parent is the Shannon-Weaver model of communication developed in the late 1940s by two mathematicians at the Bell Telephone Laboratories. The purpose of the model was to analyze the effectiveness of communication systems, like telephones, by

measuring the difference between what the source sent and
what the receiver received. If, for example, the source sent
tones up to ten thousand cycles per second, but the receiver received tones only up to six thousand cycles per second, there
was a clear loss of communication effectiveness, and you had to
send a repairman to fix the lines, or you had to select another
more efficient channel.

All of which is fine if we are measuring tones over a telephone line, but which is utterly misleading if we are measuring human communication. As we listen to a person speaking
to us, we are not pieces of electronic equipment receiving and
holding the data. We are human beings interacting with what
the speaker is saying, sifting it, debating it, adding to it. We
are thinking what we will have for lunch, wondering how
things are going at home, trying to make connections between
what is said and our own experience, thinking random
thoughts, some of which are stimulated by the speech and
some of which are imported into the situation by our own creativity. If anyone wants to assess what is happening in the
communication, let that person not try to measure how much
of the speaker's manuscript is arriving intact in the hearer's
brain. Rather, let that person feel the texture of the tapestry
speaker and hearer weave together.

What all of this means, I think, is that we should limit
how upset we get when people do not remember what we said
in the sermon, or find some meaning there which we did not
intend. Now, to be sure, when a sermon on God moving
through the world gets heard as a sermon advocating tent revivals, there is a problem with communication, but that is a
different issue from claiming that the measure of a sermon's
effectiveness is how precisely listeners can reproduce the outline. A friend of mine who attends the same church we do said
to me recently, "I understand I missed a fabulous sermon
Sunday. What was it about?"

"It was a fine sermon," I responded. "What did you hear
about it?"

"My secretary was there, and she said it was one of the

most powerful sermons she had heard in a long time, but
when I asked her about it, she couldn't remember a thing the
preacher had said."

The engineers at Bell Labs would no doubt send out a
technician to work on the lines, but a preacher may well have
reason to rejoice over a hearer who cannot recall what was
said but who is still savoring the places in her life where the
sermon made an impact, the places where she attached pieces
of her own experience to a sermonic pattern she can no longer
clearly see.

Now, let us turn to those facets of the listening process for
which we who preach do exercise some responsibility and over
which we do have some degree of control. And let us begin at
the beginning, with that moment of silence which precedes every sermon. The scripture has been read and the sermon
notes have been positioned and straightened. The preacher is
about to begin, but before there is a word, there is silence.

Almost every listener, and surely every preacher, knows
that this is not an empty silence. Most of you know well that
now-familiar, but nonetheless exquisite, passage from
Frederick Buechner's *Telling the Truth* which describes this
moment:

> So the sermon hymn comes to a close with a somewhat un-
> steady amen, and the organist gestures the choir to sit down.
> . . . [T]he preacher climbs the steps to the pulpit with . . . ser-
> mon in . . . hand. . . . In the front pews the old ladies turn up
> their hearing aids, and a young lady slips her six year old a
> Lifesaver and a Magic Marker. A college sophomore home for
> vacation, who is there because he was dragged there, slumps
> forward, his chin in his hand. The vice-president of a bank who
> twice that week has seriously contemplated suicide places his
> hymnal in the rack. A pregnant girl feels the life stir inside her.
> A high-school math teacher, who for twenty years has managed
> to keep his homosexuality a secret for the most part even from
> himself, creases his order of service down the center with his
> thumbnail and tucks it under his knee. . . . The preacher pulls
> the little cord that turns on the lectern light and deals out his
> note cards like a riverboat gambler. The stakes have never been
> higher. Two minutes from now he may have lost his listeners

completely to their own thoughts, but at this minute he has them
in the palm of his hand. The silence in the shabby church is deaf-
ening because everybody is listening to it. Everybody is listening
including even himself. Everybody knows the kind of things he
has told them before and not told them, but who knows what this
time, out of the silence, he will tell them?[2]

Buechner, in the beauty of his expression, points to the
significance of this silent moment. Karl Barth reaches its
depths more fully when he says

> On Sunday morning when the bells ring to call the congrega-
> tion and minister to worship, there is in the air an *expectancy*
> that something great, crucial, and momentous is to
> happen. . . . "God is present!" God *is* present. The whole situa-
> tion witnesses, cries, simply shouts of it, even when in minis-
> ter or people there arises questioning, wretchedness, or
> despair. . . . And [the people] want to find out and thoroughly
> understand the answer to this one question, *Is it true?*[3]

Buechner and Barth, each in their own way, are reminding us that the listening has begun before we speak, and that
the listening beginning even in this silent moment is not
formless and void, but is shaped by a profound sense of ex-
pectancy. What is missing from Buechner's scene and present
only in muted form in the passage from Barth is that the ones
doing the listening in this moment are the *church*. They are
the restless church, the doubting church, the lukewarm
church, even, at times, the faithless church, but they are the
church. They are the church of the wheat and the tares, an in-
escapable alloy of loyalty and desertion, servanthood and pre-
tense, but they *are* the church, the body of Jesus Christ. This
is not romanticism; this is theological perception. Barth, in
another place, claims that for the church to affirm, "I believe
in the Holy Catholic Church," is to say that

> at this place, in this assembly, the work of the Holy Spirit
> takes place. . . . [T]he church is not the object of faith. We do
> not believe in the church; but we do believe that in this con-
> gregation the work of the Holy Spirit becomes an event.[4]

The fact that those who listen now in silence are the

church nuances this moment in many ways. Let me name two. First, these are people who have heard the Word before and in some way built their lives around it. They have "ears to hear," and they have heard. This means that we who preach do not have the whole gospel in our grasp ready to drop it into empty vessels. Our task is not simply to proclaim the gospel *to* them, but to recognize it *in* them as well, to name it, celebrate it, nurture and guide it. Fred Craddock understands it best, I think, when he observes that preachers are not only to tell people what they need to hear but also to say what they would like to say.[5]

Second, the fact that they who listen are the church defines our relationship to them. We are not Amos, charging unannounced and uninvited into Bethel with a word from the Lord. We are to preach the word of Amos, but we stand *under* that word, and we preach as the one chosen by them to speak it. We stood among them. They laid hands upon us and, with prayer, set us apart for this ministry. They send us to their Scripture, ask that we listen to that Scripture on their behalf, and now they trust us to tell them the truth about what we have encountered there. In that moment of silence before we speak, our ordination is dynamically reaffirmed by their listening.

We can, of course, damage that moment by thinking we have no authority and trying to manufacture it by intimidating them or by using that authority to bully them or by running from the pressure of that authority. Occasionally in my teaching I find students who do not want to preach from the pulpit. They view the pulpit as elevating the clergy in an oppressive fashion, and they prefer to preach down on the level with the congregation. Much can be said for that style, of course, especially on certain occasions, but it always makes me wonder whether the student is really responding to democracy or whether the student has suddenly felt the awe-ful demands of the authority and responsibility genuinely present in the preaching moment itself and is searching for some relief.

The presence of an increasing number of women in the ministry has been accompanied by a renewed examination of the concept of authority in preaching. Many women ministers report not only that they experience authority in preaching in ways which differ from those traditionally described by their male colleagues, but also that they reject the idea that authority for ministry grows from such presumed sources as power and status. This conversation about authority is, in many ways, just beginning in earnest, and all the places it may lead cannot be foreseen. It does seem to me, though, that the discussion holds real promise for clarifying the *location* of authority in preaching. Authority in preaching resides essentially in the event, not in the person or the office of the preacher. We may speak meaningfully of the authority of the preacher, of course, but only if we remember that such authority is always derived from the dynamic relationship between the preacher and the eventfulness of the preaching act.

In the silence that inaugurates the preaching moment, we are given again permission to minister, permission to speak, and now we must speak. The sermon must begin. What should the opening of a sermon be like? Are there guidelines to follow in the introductions of sermons? George Buttrick used to say that sermons should have introductions which are (1) brief, (2) interesting, and (3) raise the issue. That is pretty good, but Buttrick's formula, in my view, is a near miss.

First of all, should sermon introductions be brief? Most of the time, probably so, but not necessarily. The opening sections of sermons have some communicational work to do, and they should take no more or no less time than is necessary getting that work done. The goal is to know what you are trying to do in the introduction and to do it. In most sermons, this can be done quickly, and should be, but sometimes it takes longer to set up the sermon.

Should introductions be interesting? Well, if the alternative is dullness, then, yes, they should be interesting, but there is a trap here. Sometimes we preachers interpret this guideline to mean that the task of the introduction is to grab people's attention, so we try to create introductions which startle, dazzle, and amaze. I am told that a certain histrionic evangelist would sometimes roar down the center aisle on a motorcycle, leap off, and shout, "You're all going to hell!" Now, that is interesting, but like many glitzy sermon introductions I have heard, it promises more than it can deliver. Randall Nichols is surely correct when he writes:

> Time after time we have heard that the purpose of an introduction is to "get people's attention." Now really, when was the last time anyone saw a preacher step into the pulpit at sermon time and *not* have everyone's attention? The rather more painful fact is that we already have their attention and their willingness as a free gift—for a while.[6]

The task of an introduction, then, is not to get their attention, but rather not to lose it. And that fact gets us at the heart of the communicational work an introduction is supposed to do. Buttrick says it should "raise the issue" of the sermon, but that too easily slips into the shopworn notion that we are supposed to "tell 'em what we gonna tell 'em," and then in the body of the sermon we "tell 'em," and in the conclusion we "tell 'em what we told 'em." The communicational task of the introduction is not to "tell 'em what you're gonna tell 'em," but rather to make promises to them about what will happen in the sermon.

Now do not take this too literally. This does not mean that we stand up and say, "Listen to this sermon, and I promise that before it's over such and such will happen." Those are not the words we use, but that is as a matter of fact what is happening. When we consider how people use their ears, how human beings listen to messages, we know that people listen to us faster than we can talk. A professional baseball player once reported that the first lesson of running the basepaths is to learn that you cannot outrun the ball. Just so, one of the first lessons of speaking is that you cannot outrun the listener. The listener is taking what we say and, on the basis of that, guessing where we are going and running out ahead to that spot to meet us. The sermon introduction hints to the listeners where to go down the road and promises that we will be there to meet them.

Take, for example, the following introduction from a published sermon:

> The story of Noah and his ark is not something we grownups take very seriously. We tend to regard it as a story for children, and we have our children making replicas of the ark in Sunday school. But it is a very strange thing really, that we should regard this as a children's story (which is to say a fairy tale), because it is a dark and frightening story. Furthermore, it is a story about ourselves and our world—a story which is quite modern.[7]

Now, I would submit that among the several important questions to ask about that introduction, the *most* important is, "What promises would a reasonable listener find there?" It seems to me clear that what this preacher is promising is that, when this sermon is said and done, the preacher will have helped the hearers to take the Noah story more seriously by exposing its "dark and frightening side" and by connecting it to real issues in contemporary life.

Is this a *good* introduction? We cannot tell yet. If this preacher does not keep his promises, then the introduction was misleading, and he broke covenant with his congregation.

Let me summarize this discussion of introductions by being so bold as to replace Dr. Buttrick's three rules with three of my own:

1. *A sermon introduction should make, implicitly or explicitly, at least one promise which the hearers would like to see kept.* The point here is not to try to figure out whether we are, or are not, making a promise in the beginning of a sermon; we are doing that whether we want to or not. The point is to make sure that the promises we *are* making are ones that the hearers will care about.

See what you think about this sermon introduction:

> Last Thursday was an important day for the church, and yet it passed most of us by unnoticed. We did not circle the date on our calendars in red, and even though it was a holiday nobody stayed home from work or cooked a turkey in celebration. The day we missed was Ascension Day, the day when the church

remembers Jesus ascending into heaven. How did we lose the importance of that day, and how can we restore its meaning?

To employ Buttrick again, that introduction is brief, fairly interesting, and it certainly raises an issue. The problem with it is that it promises to pursue an issue about which most people could not care less. The listener's mind races ahead of the preacher, guessing—perhaps accurately—that this sermon promises twenty minutes of thrashing around in obscure matters. Most hearers will probably choose to let the preacher take that journey alone.

Does this mean, then, that we can have introductions and therefore preach only about things in which people are already interested? Some homileticians think so, and they will give advice like, "Begin where the people are." That is a half-truth at best. We can preach, indeed we have a responsibility to preach, on many themes which people, because of indifference or resistance, would not at first want to hear about, even a theme like the Ascension. But we can preach on these—and this is the key—we preach on these because we have discovered them to be crucial to the living out of the Christian life, and if this is so, we should promise this in the introduction.

To go back to our Ascension Day preacher, he has chosen to preach that sermon because he no doubt is convinced that a proper relationship to the Ascension makes some kind of real difference. It changes the way we understand ourselves and God; it alters the way we see the world, and the choices we make in it. If this is not so, the sermon should be scrapped. If it is so, then some hint about that should be given to the hearer in the introduction. "Go with me on this sermon journey," invites the introduction. "It will make a difference to you. I promise."

The second rule about introductions is this:

2. *Make the promise to the hearers fairly early in the sermon.* If the introduction is brief, then there is no problem here. Suppose, however, you are introducing your sermon with a fairly long description of the social conditions of Israel in the eighth century B.C. Nothing is wrong with that; it is a

good way to start a sermon on some prophetic texts. Nothing is wrong with that as long as we keep in mind that there is a limit to how long a hearer will suspend the question, "What does this have to do with me?" We listen to messages looking for what this has to say to us, which may sound like selfishness, but is really just the acknowledgement that we cannot listen for someone else; we can only listen for ourselves.

If we are talking about the eighth century B.C. we can accomplish this connection with the listener in two main ways. If we are skillful enough, we can do this implicitly by describing the eighth century in such a way that the listener says, "That sounds like what I read in the paper this morning." Alternatively, we can be more explicit, saying that what Amos found in Israel, he would still find in Washington or Knoxville; what he saw in the sanctuary at Bethel, he would see in many churches; and that what he told them then still has the power to outrage us—or to save us.

The final rule about introductions is short and direct:

3. *Keep your promises.* If we lead people, on the basis of the introduction, to believe that we are going to do something in the sermon, it is a betrayal of trust not to do it. I am not talking about the sermon in which preacher and congregation anguish together toward a goal they finally are not able to reach. I am talking about the introduction which teases the congregation into listening by setting up a situation which is then ducked or trivialized by the sermon.

Consider this introduction from a well-known preacher:

> You can have power over all your difficulties. It is quite easy, is it not, to make such a statement. But think of the tremendous, overwhelming implications of the words! Consider the difficulties to which human beings are prone, and then consider my audacity in saying it. Yet, I repeat, you can have power over all your difficulties.[8]

Now this preacher is clearly not going to be able to deliver what he is promising. I am fully aware that what this preacher may do is to pull a presto-change-o in the sermon and substitute new and theological definitions for ordinary words like "power" and "difficulties," but a careful listener will probably feel "had" by that process. Moreover, there is not a hint of that in the introduction, no warning that we can have power over all our difficulties only if we see "power" from a certain perspective. He is arresting people's interest by promising something he cannot do.

You may say, "So what?" Listeners are not stupid; they do not expect such a promise to be met. It at least keeps their interest and they will play the game to the end and probably get something helpful from the sermon. I would simply respond by saying that speaking the truth is what preaching is about, and the fabric of trust necessary for the speaking of truth can stand only so many assaults.

In some ways this is like the experience of an acquaintance of mine who told a powerful story in one of his sermons. After the service, a man approached him, obviously moved by the story and concerned about one of the persons involved. The preacher reassured him all was well, since he had actually made up the story. The man felt betrayed by the preacher and was outraged. And well he should have been. It is fine to make up sermon stories, and a case can even be made for a certain degree of poetic finesse in all storytelling, but hearers have the right to know when they are being treated to an outright fiction. The preacher protested that the factualness of the story was not the issue; the point of the story was still true. That did not soothe the man's feelings, because what had been damaged was not the point of the sermon, but the relationship of trust in which preaching takes place.

Misleading sermon introductions do not usually create a sense of betrayal and outrage, but if we throw out enough dishonest firecrackers which lead only to a fizzle, our listeners will learn to keep their emotional distance.

Something I am saying here about introductions guides me in what I want to say about the rest of the sermon. We have seen that in sermon introductions preacher and listener already participate in a high level of interaction; the pointing in a direction, the racing ahead, and the mutual meeting that happens in preaching. This is human communication, not a telephone line, and both speaker and hearer are creating the eventfulness of it. This interaction was recognized as important even as early as Augustine, who compared a sermon to a conversation in which preacher and hearer both take part. Even though the hearer's part is technically silent, it is still there, and even though the preacher exerts a high degree of control over the conversation, this control should not be coercive. Space should be made in the sermon for the hearer's voice to find expression.

Now if preaching is a type of conversation, and the introduction is a way of saying, "This is what we're going to talk about today, and if you will talk about it with me, certain things will happen," then how should the rest of the conversation proceed? I want to make several suggestions about this, and, for the sake of time, I am going to confine myself to a few issues based on what appear to me to be common problems with the sermons most of us preach.

First of all, we encounter the problem of hiding the issue, not saying exactly what we mean. I am talking here about the widespread tendency of those of us who preach to get to a place in our sermons where we are referring to a very specific issue in our common life, but, instead of naming it and saying what we mean, we retreat to the level of broad generalities, hoping the hearer will get the point without our having to name it. We speak of the "need for reconciliation in areas of pain and strife," when we really mean the recent congregational fight over the community ministry program. We say that "the gospel gives us hope in those moments when life closes in on us," when we are really talking about that diagnosis of cancer, this closing of a textile mill, or those families struggling with alcoholism.

In Anne Tyler's *Dinner at the Homesick Restaurant*, an elderly woman has died, and one of her children, Cody, is listening to the minister preach the funeral sermon. The narrator says:

> At the funeral, the minister, who had never met their mother, delivered a eulogy so vague, so general, so universally

applicable that Cody thought of that parlor game where people fill in words at random and then giggle hysterically at the story that results.[9]

Vague, general, universally applicable, these are adjectives that could be applied to many sermons. How far should we go in being direct and specific? Let us think about that for a minute. The linguist Robin Lakoff has observed that when human beings speak to each other, in addition to the desire to communicate something, they also convey the desire to be in communion with another person, the desire not to be alone.[10] We would die if we were deprived of human community, and we have developed strategies for speaking to other people in such a way that we can say what we want to say without offending, pushing away, or breaking communion. The result of this is that we often say things to people by not really saying them, but by saying something else, and hoping they will catch little signals here and there and fill in the blanks with the meaning we really intend.

Everybody does this, but different cultures have different unwritten rules for how it is to be done. As a southerner living in New Jersey, for example, I have discovered that patterns of conversation I have practiced all my life and that I believe are perfectly clear often cause my friends deep confusion. I will meet somebody on the street, chat for a few minutes, and then as we part I will add, almost unconsciously, "Come see us." This is usually greeted with a perplexed look and sometimes a weak, "Right now?" They do not understand that I am not communicating information; I am maintaining communion.

Or, listen to this rather ordinary conversation between two southerners. One of them has paid an afternoon visit to the other, and the hostess says, "Would you like something to drink?"

The other person says, "Oh no, don't go to any trouble" (which virtually every southerner knows is code for, "Yes, I would like something to drink").

The hostess, knowing the code, says, "It's no trouble. I've got coffee, tea, and Coke. What would you like?"

"Whatever you're having. Don't fix anything just for me" (which is code for, I have something in mind, but I'm not sure it's all right to ask for it).

"Oh no, the coffee's brewed, the tea water's hot, and the Coke's in the frig. It's no trouble at all."

"How nice. Well then, I'd like a cup of coffee."

"Fine. Sugar? Cream?"

"Oh, don't mess with all that" (In other words, one sugar and a little cream).

This kind of conversation drives New Jersians crazy. Ask natives of New Jersey if they would like something to drink, and they will say, "Yes, I'm thirsty. I want some juice." But it is a sign of how much we in the southern culture value the communion aspect of communication that we spend much of our time saying what we do not mean, or rather, saying what we do mean indirectly with nuances, hints, winks, and verbal inflections.

Quite apart from the cultural influence, the more people are under pressure, the more they fear that what they say may break community, the more indirect they become, the more they say what they mean by saying what they do not mean. This is where preaching comes in. Sometimes being indirect in sermons is a sign of discretion and pastoral care. We preach a word of grace to the woman whose marriage has come apart, to the teenager uncertain of his sexual identity, to the alcoholic wrestling with guilt in indirect and general language. They know we are speaking to them, but they are not singled out and they are not exposed. But sometimes we are speaking to a larger community issue which needs a clear and direct word, and we still become vague and obscure, not because of pastoral concern, but because we are afraid. I have always admired a passage in one of John Fry's sermons on the "blind Bartimaeus" text in Mark. The sermon was preached in 1969, a time of civil unrest, and a time in which the federal government had just released a controversial report on the social inequities in the cities. In the sermon, Fry had made the point that Bartimaeus' blindness was a metaphor for the stubborn blindness of the people, and then he said:

[It is in the context of this story that] we ought to read the [Congressional] commission report on civil disorders. It highlights more than all else the inability of America to conceive, even, the plight of the urban poor. America cannot see the charity situation for what it is. The situation of police brutality for what it is. The story of the deliverance of Bartimaeus should be required reading before you read the commission report. Then you have the background to understand its insistence that there is a fundamental blindness in the land. Not merely an unwillingness but an inability to see the rank disparity in the living situations of the rich to the poor. Especially the black poor. All that can be said about the plight of Bartimaeus can be transferred exactly and said exactly of the members of the Welfare Tenants Unions who spoke with such eloquence yesterday as they testified before Illinois Lawmakers down in Springfield. They talked about enforced patterns and degradation built into our charity system.[11]

Right or wrong, that was what John Fry heard from this text on Mark. It was what he had in mind, and so he said it. I think most of us retreat from direct speech too often. The result is that the listeners hear Christian rhythms in our sermons, but have to guess what we are really talking about. Everybody loves a broad sermon on "Thou shall not steal," for it is always about somebody else. But when the Heidelberg Catechism says, "Thou shalt not use false weights and measures," we are down to cases. I think we ought to look at our next sermons and ask ourselves, "What am I really talking about here? Would it be more helpful if I said what I mean?"

The second problem with the flow of conversation in preaching has to do with what has been traditionally been called "transitions," those little connecting strands between major sections of the sermon. A good bit of fun has been poked at the traditional three-point sermon, and especially at those preachers who wave a flag every time there is a shift by saying, "Now the second thing I want to tell you this morning is. . . ." As a matter of fact, the high profile point-structured sermon is actually a very serviceable design for communication. I am using it in this chapter right now, incidentally; we are on the second typical problem with sermons, if you have lost count.

The problem with the point style of preaching is not that it is evil, but that it is limited. It does only a few things well, chiefly one, the communication of systematically-related ideas. When the sermon is trying to do something else, though, like enabling a sense of discovery about something, drawing insights from a narrative, or letting one idea build upon another, a more fluid, less outline-oriented structure is much more effective.

Even when we employ a more flowing sermon form—and for good contemporary preaching, that is most of the time—we need to learn a lesson from the three-point preacher: listeners need guideposts, milestone markers, to know when the conversation has made a turn.

At our house during family dinner table conversation, sometimes something said will set my mind off on a journey. What was said reminds me of something, and that, in turn, reminds me of something else. Often the chain will proceed for several links before I blurt out the end result of my thinking. Because the linkages are in my head, though, what I say seems completely disconnected from what has been said, and at that point, my children will roll their eyes at each other and in unison shout, "Random, Dad—really random."

What this points to in terms of human communication is the well-known fact that when people are listening to us, they are not *just* listening to us, they are attempting to organize what we are saying into some meaningful whole. That means that when we say something to them that comes at them, or seems to come at them, as an idiosyncratic bank shot off the wall, it not only strikes them as "random" and irrelevant, it also frustrates the listening process. Some silent voice from deep within the listener says, "You're not cooperating with me" or "That's nonsense" or worst of all, "This is too much work to put together. I quit."

That also means that the transitions in sermons—I prefer to call them "connectors"—are not just the spacers which divide the sections; they are essential elements with crucial communicational work to accomplish.

This sounds, I know, like a small matter, but it is amazing how much mischief this kind of thing causes in preaching. Though the flow of what we are saying makes perfectly good sense to us because we know how the logic goes, it is a frequent fault in preachers not to let the hearers in on these turns and connections. The result is that what seems crystal clear to us is perceived by the hearers to be incoherent and unlistenable.

Communication experts use the term "meta-communication" to describe the process I am talking about. "Meta-communication" is communication about communication, and the whole concept refers to the way in which, as we communicate with people, we are also giving them clues and signals about how to listen to what we are saying. We raise our voices in order to imply, "Now this is urgent," or we lower them in order to say, "Now this is just between us, so listen closely." And we put in connectors to say, "Now we're going off in a little different direction here, so watch your step." Listeners want and need more of this kind of guidance than most preachers seem willing to provide.

Here is an easy test preachers can perform on their own sermons. Take a manuscript of one of your sermons. The best kind is a verbatim manuscript taken from a tape recording of the sermon as it was actually delivered. With a blue pencil draw a box around the core content of each of the sections, units, moves, points, or whatever you call the major components of the sermon. The stuff between the boxes is the transitional material, the connectors. If there is nothing there, in most cases there ought to be.

Take each of these transitional sections and submit it to a two-part test:

1. Does it refer in some way to the essence of what was said in the previous box?
2. Does it anticipate in some way the material which will follow in the next box?

Suppose, by way of illustration, a district sales manager is having a conversation over lunch with a corporate vice president, trying to convince her that their company ought to put a sales office in Memphis. After discussing the many ways in which

Memphis is growing, the sales manager then says, "So, look, Memphis is the hottest market in my district, and here's how I see a sales office taking advantage of that. . . ."

That is a connector, a marker of a turn in the conversation, and notice what it does. First, it summarizes what has just been going on in the conversation: "So, look, what I've been telling you is that Memphis is a hot market." If the vice president has been successfully following the conversation, this provides a small, but emotionally satisfying confirmation that she has heard correctly. If, on the other hand, she has been confused by the conversation, or if her mind has wandered, this rescues the conversation by bringing it back to common ground.

Then the sales manager hints at what is coming next: "A sales office in Memphis can be a winner, and here's how. . . ." That allows the vice president not only to listen *to* what her partner has to say, but also to listen *for* something in the next segment of the conversation. There are some empty hooks in her listening labeled "what a sales office can do for us," and she is now anticipating that he will provide something to hang on those hooks. By doing that, she is participating in what is said in a more active fashion.

Now, listen to this transition from a sermon, which effectively accomplishes the same things. It comes from a Christmas eve sermon, and the preacher has been talking about the joyful dimensions of that time. He says:

> It is the night, more than any other night of the year, when we experience the innermost peace of the Divine Presence among us and within us.
>
> Yet, paradoxically, it is likewise a night of sadness.[12]

That is a helpful connector because it stands at a turn in the conversation, gelling what we have just been listening to (the joyfulness of Christmas eve), and signalling what we should now be listening for (the sadness in the same occasion).

To be sure, connectors in sermons do not always have to be this full, two-part formula. Sometimes the work can be done in a single word, like, "But . . . ," or even with a silent pause that implies that what has been said is worthy of deeper thought, and that deeper thinking is what we are about to do. The work of a connector may be accomplished in many ways, but the work has to be done if people are going to integrate what we are preaching to them.

The thinking we have done thus far about how people actively listen to us leads me to the last problem in preaching I want to address. We all know that various preachers have different preaching styles, but what is not so well acknowledged is that listeners have different listening styles. If there is to be a genuine conversation between preacher and hearer in preaching then there must be a relative degree of "fit" between these two styles. Some people think that listening styles are related to educational and economic levels. I believe, rather, that they are more the product of personality distinctions and cultural patterns.

Several years ago, two linguists, Sara Michaels and Jenny Cook-Gumperz, did a study of the interaction between students and their teacher in a first grade classroom. The students had been asked by the teacher to tell the class a story, and one by one they were called to the front to spin their yarns. What the linguists discovered was that the white children in the class told their stories according to their cultural conventions about storytelling. Their stories were something like Aesop's Fables. "Once upon a time," they would begin, and after a brief narrative, voila, out would fall a moral, insight, or point. The teacher, who was also white, would clap her hands and reward them by saying what a good story that was.

Most of the black students, however, were operating out of different narrative conventions. They intuitively employed a technique called "topic chaining," one story impressionistically connecting to another story, and that to yet another, until the teacher, tired of what she perceived as just rambling, cut them off before they had the chance to make their points. From a linguistic point of view, the black students were just as skillful as the whites in employing their storytelling strategies, but their speaking style was out of phase with the teacher's listening style.[13]

So there we are on Sunday morning, standing before a congregation to preach. We have our style, our way of putting sermons together, but out there are many listening styles. What happens?

The good news is that we grow toward each other. Preachers and their hearers, over time, move toward some common middle. Slowly adjustments are made in our styles and in theirs. Listeners who cannot, or will not, do this, either wait out our ministry or find another church.

The harder news is that differences remain. If we preach in the highly poetic style of a Frederick Buechner, some highly structured listeners out there will forever complain that they just could not see what we were getting at. If, on the other hand, we preach masterpieces of organized logic, others will find our sermons dull, predictable, and aesthetically numbing.

I would encourage each of us who preach to view our personal preaching style not as a focused laser beam, always neatly cutting the same groove, but as a spectrum of possibilities. None of us can assume just any style we want, but each of us has a range of possibilities worth exploring. The tendency is to fall into a rut, cutting every sermon according to the same pattern. If, for example, we prefer that poetic style, we ought self-consciously to create an occasional sermon with a more tightly organized structure. We can, if we wish, let the biblical texts call some of the shots here. Some texts demand the fluid, the experiential, the poetic style. Others come at us more straightforwardly. But if we can shift our styles within a reasonable range, the result will be that people in our congregations who had only been eavesdropping on our sermons will suddenly find their ears opened and their lives addressed.

Chapter 4

The Embodiment of Preaching

I was cruising down a rural highway one oven-baked June Sunday, the radio blasting and my mind on the cool mountains and the few days of rest which lay ahead. The station began to fade, and I twisted the dial to find another. As I did, I discovered that I had just passed through a time zone, not from Eastern Standard to Central Standard, but from profane to sacred. It was now 11:00 A.M., the customary time for worship in that part of the world, and, on station after station, the Beatles had now yielded to First Baptist and Madonna to Macedonia Methodist. Rather than settling in on one service, I moved the dial back and forth, tasting the available varieties: a Whitman's Sampler of small-town Protestantism.

What I heard almost drove me to the conclusion that services of worship should never, under any circumstances, be broadcast on the radio. It was like listening through the wall to a drab party in the apartment next door: you just hoped they were having more fun in there than it sounded. I heard a thundering pipe organ steamroll a congregation into submission with the "Gloria." I heard an associate pastor gather the children around for a children's sermon which employed an analogical object lesson so complex T. S. Eliot could not have made the cognitive leap. I heard several murmured recitations of the

Apostles' Creed, each uttered with the cheerlessness of a farm market report. As I flipped around the dial, I heard Presbyterians, Lutherans, Methodists, and Baptists coughing, bumping the pews, thudding hymnbooks into the racks, and making all the noises of people longing for release.

Now, I know that I am not being fair. The worth of worship cannot be evaluated at a distance. A person in a knit shirt heading down the road toward a vacation has little right or perspective to make judgments about the overheard services of other people. You have to be there. Regular worship, like regular family conversation, does not often make good theater, but it shapes and nourishes people nonetheless.

I suspect, though, that something of my reaction to what I heard would be shared by the people who were there in those sanctuaries that morning. There is a blandness about much of worship, especially in midstream Protestantism. A student of mine once reported that what she found objectionable about most worship was that "it is such bad drama." I raised an immediate caveat about confusing worship with the performing arts, but, down deep, I knew what she meant, and I knew she was right. Worship may not provide a good show for spectators, but it should possess dramatic strength for the participants. We gather to celebrate the central mystery of the universe. We have as resources liturgical texts of immense grandeur and poetic vigor. Properly understood, a well-crafted order of worship moves with ritual power. Yet, we often walk through it with all the excitement and dramatic sensitivity of clerks in the post office.

As surprising as it may sound, a malaise in worship eventually infects preaching as well. I say "surprising," because it is widely held that preaching thrives at the expense of the rest of the liturgy, that nonchalance about matters liturgical is a direct result of an overemphasis upon preaching as the centerpiece of worship. The evidence for this is the fact that, with a few exceptions, those traditions which place a premium upon preaching tend to be more casual about the rest of worship, and *vice versa*. There is something to this, of course. My own tradition, Reformed, invented the phrase "aller au sermon" (roughly, "going to preaching") as a shorthand notation for the whole of worship and has struggled ever since to understand the liturgy as anything more than a set piece for preaching. The fact of the matter, however, is that Sunday preaching is *embodied* in and through the liturgy, bound sinew and bone to the other elements of worship. A deadness in worship will sooner or later drain the life from even the best of preaching. Conversely, liturgy which lacks energetic attention to preaching will almost inevitably drift toward being obscure, quietist, and closed to the world. Preaching and liturgy do not exist in isolation wards, and a disease in one finally saps the strength from the other.

Our goal is to describe the kind of relationship which ought to exist between the sermon and the rest of worship. Before this can be done, though, we need to examine the nature of Christian worship in general. In *Doxology,* the liturgical theologian Geoffrey Wainwright formulated the following description of Christian worship: worship is "the point of concentration at which the whole of the Christian life comes to ritual focus."[1] Three observations flow from Wainwright's statement:

1. *Worship is the point of concentration . . .* This does not mean, of course, that worship, in a formal sense, is *all* that Christians do, but it does mean that everything Christians do is *grounded* in the act of worship. Worship is not simply a "program," one of the many activities of the church; it is the *essential* activity from which all other actions flow and to which all others return.

It is difficult to overstate the importance of this concept of worship to the life of the church. It is far more than a question of where to place the worship committee on the congregational organizational chart. It has to do, frankly, with whether we are functional theists or a-theists. To put it bluntly, either God is or God is not. There is either the Burning Bush calling us to be God's people, or there is merely wishful thinking reflected in the glint of the sun on the shrub. Either an angel speaks, or the sky simply thunders. Barth's picture of the Sunday service is apt, the entire event crying out that God is present and the congregation silently speaking the urgent question, "Is it true?" If it is true, then the crucial human action, the central deed without which human life in any full sense is not possible, is falling before this Mystery in worship. If it is not true, then the *New York Times* crossword puzzle is Sunday's best and deepest mystery.

One day I found myself in the audience at a panel discussion about campus ministry. The panel was made of the team of chaplains from a nearby university; several Protestant ministers, two priests, and one rabbi. A man got up from his chair to ask the panel one of those impossibly open-ended questions such occasions seem to invite: "Tell me what today's university students are like." The panel members glanced at each other with a who-wants-to-field-this-one look. Finally one of the ministers gave it a try. "I think you'd be pleased by the attitudes on campus these days." This chaplain went on to describe how, in the midst of the undeniable careerism and financial ambitions of contemporary students, an admirable and unselfish volunteer spirit was also emerging. Cases were cited of students who were giving their time to nursing homes, soup kitchens, and causes like divestiture in South Africa.

As this speech progressed, the rabbi on the panel began to smile quietly, then to grin widely. Distracted, the minister turned to the rabbi and asked, "Am I saying something funny?"

"No, not really," replied the rabbi. "What you are saying is that the students are good people. And they are. You're saying that they do good things. And they do. I was just thinking, though, that the one thing they lack is a vision of *salvation.*"

We all looked at the rabbi. He then went on to explain his own conviction that ethical impulses cannot be sustained on good intentions alone. The problems persist, and the flame of idealism finally burns itself out on discouragement. Perseverance in ethical action, he insisted, depends upon maintaining some vision of what God is doing in the world, a vision that embraces but also transcends our own efforts—in short, a vision of salvation.

It is precisely such a vision, a vision of what God has done, is doing, and will do in the world, which lies at the heart of worship. In this vision, the Christian life finds its center, its point of concentration. Without it, the Christian life is simply unthinkable.

2. . . . *at which the whole of the Christian life* . . . Metaphorically, at least, the doors of the sanctuary, like those in saloons, ought to be swinging doors. What happens in worship ought to flow into the world, and the mission of the church to the world ought to find expression in worship. Christian worship and Christian mission are in dialectical relationship. This means that, on the one hand, worship and service are not the same thing, and they cannot be collapsed into each other, but on the other hand, they cannot be separated either.

The common bulletin slogan "Enter to Worship; Depart to Serve" rings with a certain truthfulness, but it is only a half-truth because it draws the distinction between worship and service too sharply. The medieval monastic saying *"laborare est orare; orare est laborare"* ("to work is to pray; to pray is to work") is perhaps closer to the full truth, but it runs the danger of blurring the necessary distinction.[2] It is better to say that every act of worship is incomplete unless it leads explicitly to some form of Christian action in the world, and every form of Christian action in the world is incomplete unless it leads to some explicit expression of praise. To sing in the sanctuary, "The earth is the Lord's and the fullness thereof," should release energy for the care of the earth. Likewise, caring for the earth should lead finally to the prayerful cry, "The earth is the Lord's and the fullness thereof."

When I was a boy I worshiped in a small Georgia church set in a village. One warm summer Sunday we were observing the Lord's Supper, and, in those pre-air-conditioned days, the windows were open to catch the occasional breeze. As the minister read the familiar words, "For I received from the Lord what I also delivered to you," we could hear sounds from the outside: birds singing, muffled conversation coming from a neighboring house, the passing of a car. When the supper had been served, the minister started to replace the silver covers for the trays, but then paused. "Has everyone been fed?" he asked. No one responded, and his hand started again toward the tray. The he paused a second time, and, in a voice more firm and urgent, he said, "Has *everyone* been fed?" The congregation grew breathlessly still, uncertain of the reason for his hesitancy to conclude the sacrament. Outside were the sounds of an engine starting, someone laughing, the cry of a baby. "Has everyone been fed?" Only gradually in that silent moment did we realize that the minister's question echoed beyond the walls of the little sanctuary, out into the world of many hungers, and that this supper would not be finished until truly *everyone* had been fed.

3. . . . *comes to ritual focus.* A service of worship is a *ritual,* and it is both a positive and a negative mark of our culture that the word "ritual" has to be defended. We are rightly suspicious of tiresome and vacant ceremonies, "mere rituals," disconnected from lived experience, long on pomp and short on circumstance. On the other hand, we are a ritually impoverished people, condemned to live on the quivering surface of every event, possessing no lens to see the depths, no framework for cumulative memory. A culture that can move its national holidays around to make for long weekends has a sense of consumable time, but not of sacred time.

Simply put, a ritual is a pattern of relatively fixed and repeated actions which originates in and gains its shape from some deeply formative experience. Barbecue, fireworks, and a parade constitute the ritual; the declaring of national independence is the formative event. Candles, cake, and "Happy Birthday to You" constitute the ritual; birth is the formative event. Rituals can become dead metaphors. When they no longer evoke an active memory of the primary event, they become empty ceremonies. When, on the other hand, people have no living rituals, they have no rich corporate memory.

A number of years ago now, my high school class observed our twentieth reunion. We rented a hotel ballroom reminiscent of the one in which we held our senior prom. We decorated the room with crepe paper of red and black, our school colors, and we stocked a juke box with vintage records. We coaxed a number of our former teachers out of retirement to serve as honorary "chaperones." At the appointed time, we arrived. Some of the men were wearing penny loafers, our colorful socks matching the pastel shirts into which we had managed to squeeze our middle-aged girths. Some of the women sported bouffant hairdos and Villager outfits complete with gold circle pins. We greeted each other with phrases we had not spoken in twenty years, while, from the juke box, Danny and the Juniors sang through their noses, "You can rock it, you can roll it, you can bop it, you can stroll it, at the hop, hop, hop."

Now what were we doing? High school was never like that, not really. We had stylized bits and pieces of our school memories and fitted them into a ritual action. We had taken the music, the language, the symbols, the clothing from five years of adolescent life and compressed them into a single moment of ritual time in the hope that, by walking the walk and talking the talk of an earlier era, something of the experience of that time could be evoked.

In many ways, the ritual of worship is like that. We wear special clothing, we sing special songs, we display special colors and symbols, we employ special words and gestures, call people to fulfill special roles. By doing so we reenact, in a compressed fashion, the whole history of the people of God. In the call to worship the burning bush flames once again, the words "follow me" are voiced once more. As the Bible is opened and read, Sinai is revisited. As the bread is broken, the upper room is filled once again, the great marriage feast anticipated.

The difference is this: in a high school reunion, we are left to our own devices; in worship we are not left alone. In an ordinary ritual, *we* evoke whatever power and presence are there. In worship, we walk the walk and talk the talk because of what God has already done and in the constant prayer that God will journey with us again and speak to us anew. If that prayer is not uttered, then worship is merely a pageant. When that prayer is answered by the silence of God, then worship must be a faithful waiting for God. When God mercifully hears our cry, then worship becomes a grace-filled encounter.

This points to what is wrong with much that passes for innovation in worship. The problem is not with aspects of worship that are new, or even "experimental." Because we worship a living God, our patterns of worship are properly always evolving. Moreover, worship ought to possess something of the dramatic intensity and reflect the intrinsic excitement of the events calling it into being. The problem comes from those strategies in worship that are evidence of our weariness in waiting for God; that are, in effect, substitutes *for* God. Tired of waiting for God, we dim the rheostats to create the mood of holiness. Tired of waiting for God, we transform the call to worship from "Our help is in the name of the Lord" into "Good Morning!" At least *we* are here to greet each other. Tired of waiting for God, we "perform" anthems, display the flag, celebrate the arts, give motivational talks, spout psychobabble, use worship to promote utilitarian causes, and otherwise stroke golden calves. The problem with most gimmicks designed to infuse some excitement into worship is not that they are trendy, but that they are, at root, signs that we believe that, even in worship, we have been left to our own devices.

The understanding of liturgy as ritual also points up an interesting paradox in our worship life: we are to take what we do in worship with utmost seriousness and, at the same time, with a grain of salt. To take worship seriously is, first of all, to respect the dramatic integrity of the ritual. Rituals are not made out of disconnected gestures. They have sequence, movement, even plot. They make human, theological, and dramatic sense. The best of our rituals often possess a wisdom greater than that which readily appears on the surface.

As a lighthearted example, take the "seventh inning stretch" at a baseball game. This little piece of ritual action is no doubt completely opaque to novices and tourists from foreign shores. Suddenly thousands of people, who for six and one-half innings have been watching the game and periodically moving up and down the aisles in search of restrooms, hot dogs, and peanuts, stand in unison and sing "Take Me Out to the Ballgame" to the accompaniment of a Hammond organ. Now a behavioral psychologist may quickly sniff out that this strange custom had its origins in an easily determinable biological need, namely the desire of the human body to change positions after about two hours of sitting. A particularly pragmatic behavioral psychologist might even suggest that it is silly to assume that everyone needs relief at the same time and that it would make much better sense to decree that people should stretch whenever they desired. Such a suggestion, however, would miss the point (and could start a fistfight). Yes, the seventh inning stretch has to do with bodily needs. It also has to do with celebrating the common experience of watching a baseball game, with the evocation of childhood, with the historical continuity of baseball, and with many other things too difficult to explain to a behavioral psychologist.

So it is with orders of worship. Wisdom lies beneath the surface of ritual form. If, in a classical worship order, the creed follows the sermon, this placement is not arbitrary. It has to do with the re-creation of the church, the community of faith, by and in response to the Word. It has to do with the ancient furrows being sown once again with the seed of the gospel, and the faith which grows from that. The creed could, of course, be placed before the sermon rather than after it, but that would be a different ritual. It would speak a different truth about the relationship between Word and faith and, over time, it would shape the church's identity in a different way.

This notion that ritual form and order must be respected is an especially important lesson for the so-called "free church" liturgical tradition. There are many "free church" congregations whose order of service appears to have been constructed by writing the names of liturgical elements, like "hymn," "prayer of thanksgiving," and "offering," on slips of paper, shaking them up in a bag, and then spilling them out in random order onto the bulletin. If there is any vision of the whole at work, it seems motivated by an interior decorator's mindset ("This hymn goes with this sermon rather nicely, don't you think?"). When the dramatic shape of worship is lost, too often the sense of movement must come from the charisma of the worship leader, who is condemned to a bottomless pit of artificial enthusiasm and to endless liturgical improvisations. Improvisations have their place, of course, but working with the classical forms of liturgy is somewhat akin to singing Handel's *Messiah:* it is generally best to respect the material.

While it is certainly true that there is no one proper way to worship, it is also true that some ways are better than others. Orders of worship which consist of a line of elements like beads without a string simply provide no sense of movement. One way to test the dramatic integrity of an order of worship is to try to turn the sequence of elements into a narrative. "First God spoke, calling us to worship. Overwhelmed by God's presence, we sang a song of awe and praise, but even as we did we became aware of our unworthiness to do so, and so we confessed our sin . . . ," and so on. If the structure of the service cannot be expressed in a story, then the sequence of events is probably misplaced. If it *can* be expressed in a story, then the participants ought to be able to move through that service in such a way that the acting out of this story is manifest.

Even in those congregations where the order of service has good dramatic structure, education is necessary to bring this into awareness. When the houselights of a Broadway theater are dimmed, and the members of the audience return to their seats after the intermission, they do so remembering what has happened thus far in the play, sensing that the action remains unresolved, and anticipating the denouement which is to come. The interlude between acts is not empty, but filled with expectation. Something of the same suspense ought to fill the spaces between elements in an order of worship, and if this is to happen, worshipers need to be educated about the dramatic shape of worship.

Another aspect of taking what we do in worship seriously has to do with what has been called "presidential style," which refers to the spirit and manner in which the worship leader conducts worship. It is something of a misnomer actually, since an effective presidential style has more to do with awareness of what one is doing and a sense of place than it does with stylistic technique. It is also not confined to the one who presides. It may be most visible in the worship leader, but it also can be seen in all others who participate.

The issue here is that one embodies, in voice, in posture, and in gesture, one's sense of the true nature of the occasion. A person coming into a room for an important job interview carries herself differently than she would if she were coming into a room to adjust the thermostat. A person generally walks into Notre Dame Cathedral more slowly and with a greater sense of awe than he does sauntering into a fast food restaurant. People approach a person in a hospital bed dying of cancer with more deference than they do the ticket-taker at the movies. Our manner gives away our awareness of occasion and place.

Just so, leaders and participants in worship reveal, by their manner, their sense of occasion and place. If a worship leader is infected with an exalted sense of clericalism, it shows. If a worship leader believes that the sermon is the only important thing happening this morning, it shows. Every Christian Sunday is an Easter, which Lesslie Newbigin described as the "perpetual praise of God who not only creates order out of chaos, but breaks through fixed orders to create . . . surprise and joy."[3] If a worship leader lacks an awareness of the orderliness of worship on the one hand, or, on the other hand, shuffles through the bulletin clearly expecting no surprises, it shows.

I once knew a layman, a farmer, who, during his church's prayer meeting, would stand to pray, grip the back of the pew ahead of him with his big, gnarled hands, stand silently for a moment, and then begin, "Lord, we need rain. You *know* we need rain. We ain't had no rain since June, but even if we don't get no rain, Lord, we rest in your wisdom." Now that rough prayer will win no liturgical Pulitzers, but the man's language, posture, and tone revealed a person who genuinely believed himself to be in the presence of God. It was a holy moment to join him in prayer. Far beyond issues of technique, what we believe to be happening in worship clearly shows.

If there was a common flaw in those services I overheard on the radio, it would be in this area of presidential style. Judging by the monotony that came over the air, the worship leaders exposed their belief that they were in the presence of people to be amused, organizations to be maintained, agendas to be completed, people to be taught and persuaded, tasks to be done—but the leaders of these services communicated little sense of mystery or wonder. Nothing important was really happening in worship, because there was little expressed consciousness of a source from which any meaningful event could spring. The organist may have played too aggressively. The children's sermon may have overreached cognitively. But these were not the main problems. It is certainly ironic, and perhaps too harsh, to say it, I know, but the key dimension which seemed missing from those services was an awareness of the presence of God. As Frederick Buechner said somewhere, "God was, of all the missing persons, the most missed."

Having said all of this about the need to take worship rituals seriously, it is also true that they must be taken with a grain of salt lest we forget that the true miracle of worship is not that we are able to execute the service with flawless precision, but that God is willing to meet us here at all. It is easy to slip from the desire to worship well because God is with us to the presumption that God is with us because we have worshiped well. The former creates a faithful quest for excellence; the latter constitutes a vain attempt to perform magic.

Perhaps you, as I, have been the occasional victim at one of those stiff dinner parties where proper etiquette is not the medium; it is the message. Each place setting is complete with enough specialized silverware to perform an appendectomy. The hostess must be discreetly, but constantly, watched in order to determine which obscure utensil is to be matched with which equally mysterious dish to avoid embarrassment. Conversation proceeds with excruciating correctness.

The clock ticks. A dollop of gravy inadvertently dropped onto the tablecloth receives no mention, only the hostess' slight glance of disapproval, but this slip produces internal guilt of Kafkaesque proportions. The clock ticks. Finally the guests are paroled, their departure formalized by polite thank-yous and good-byes.

Contrast this to the dinner party where the hostess creates a space of warm hospitality. People relax, conversation moves spontaneously, jokes are told, spirits are renewed. Chances are that, even at this party, correct etiquette has been observed. No one has rolled a line of peas into his mouth with a knife. No one has made a thumb puppet with her napkin. The courses of the meal have been served in proper order. But even though the ritual has been correct in every way, it has not drawn attention to itself. The ritual has served as a vehicle for the more important matter of human interchange and has, therefore, been absorbed into that interchange. Humanity was not made for the sabbath, but the sabbath for humanity.

It is difficult to draw the line between doing liturgy with loving care and being self-conscious about doing liturgy, but the line is there, nonetheless. Worship is like a dance. It is necessary to learn the proper steps, even to practice them, and to observe the rhythm of the music. It is more important, though, to give oneself with abandon to the dance, to be so prepared that the mechanics can be forgotten in the act of joining in harmony with one's partner. The grace of worship is not that we are able to dance so well, but that God deigns to circle the floor with us in the first place.

In *Teaching a Stone to Talk,* the essayist Annie Dillard captures well the grain-of-salt perspective essential to genuine worship:

> It is the second Sunday in Advent. For a year I have been attending Mass at this Catholic church. Every Sunday for a year I have run away from home and joined the circus as a dancing bear. We dancing bears have dressed ourselves in buttoned clothes; we mince around the rings on two feet.

. . . A high school stage play is more polished than this service we have been rehearsing since the year one. In two thousand years, we have not worked out the kinks. We positively glorify them. Week after week we witness the same miracle: that God is so mighty he can stifle his own laughter. Week after week, we witness the same miracle: that God, for reasons unfathomable, refrains from blowing our dancing bear act to smithereens. Week after week Christ washes the disciples' dirty feet, handles their very toes, and repeats, It is all right—believe it or not—to be people.[4]

Dillard has it just right. There is something grand about the drama of worship taken seriously. Human voices joined in a concert of praise, the offering of the best we have in art, language, music, and dramatic gesture—there is a majesty to this. There is also something touchingly amusing about it all, something that can only be taken with a grain of salt; that is, the putting of words about God—even words *from* God—into our mouths and the parade of singers and actors who have been cast into roles too large and demanding for them. When the community led by John Calvin published one of the first of the metrical psalters in French, the preface of this book indicated that it was for all "amateurs" of the Word of God. The word meant "lovers," of course, but, in the modern context, it also means, well, amateurs. It is in both of those senses, as lovers and as amateurs of the Word of God, that we worship.

When my brother and I were children we once planned a special observance for Mother's Day. We knocked on our parents' bedroom door at first light and, when admitted, entered with the Sunday paper and the announcement that, today being a special day, breakfast would be served to them in bed. As our surprised, but pleased, parents leafed through the newspaper, they were serenaded by the homey kitchen sounds of their breakfast being prepared: glass shattering, grease fires being extinguished, reams of paper towels being spun off the roll. At long last we returned to their room with a steaming breakfast of defiant coffee, molten eggs, carbonized bacon, and biscuits which would have rivaled an apprentice stonemason. If that meal had been served at San Quentin, it would have precipitated a riot. But our parents savored every morsel, seasoning their food with the spice of long-suffering love. Inept as we were at cooking, we had so obviously prepared that meal with respect and devotion that, even though they surely found it virtually undigestible, they still counted it among their most beloved dining experiences. Somehow I believe that worship is just this way: often half-baked or overdone, but when entered into with care and devotion, graciously received and even savored by our long-suffering God.

Now how is it that preaching becomes embodied in worship? What is the place of the sermon in the overall drama of the Sunday liturgy? The place to begin is with the concept of ritual. As we noted in an earlier chapter, preaching is itself ritual activity, and therefore it has meaning not only because of what is said in the sermon, but also by virtue of the fact that a sermon is spoken at all. Week after week, a person called to the task enters the pulpit, reads a passage of Scripture, and then speaks more words—sermon words—which are an attempt to bear witness to the continuing truth in that Scripture. The sermon may be powerful or weak, interesting or dull, beautifully-crafted or flat-footed, but regardless of its intrinsic quality, it ritually enacts an impressive theological claim: we live in a world where God speaks. In a culture which expects its gods, if they exist at all, to remain distant and silent, the objects of our placid contemplation, it is wondrously disquieting to bump into a deity who disturbs the peace with talk, who wishes communion with us, who calls to us and makes claims upon our lives. "The sheep follow him, for they know his voice."

Another way of putting this is to say that the act of preaching in a service of worship (not the content of the sermon, but the very deed of speaking and listening to a sermon) is like going to the mailbox every day to see if any mail has come. Some days the box is empty. Other days the box is filled with mass-circulation flyers marked "Occupant." But we keep going, day after day, because occasionally we find something addressed to us, something personal with our own name on the envelope. Going to that mailbox is more than a habit. It is a daily ritual that evinces conviction that, somewhere out there, someone wishes to communicate with me, and eventually will do so. When people gather to listen to a sermon, they show that same confidence. Even when the box is empty today, they come again, acting out their faith that we live in a world with a God who eventually breaks the silence—and speaks.

Preaching the sermon is not only a ritual action in its own right; it is also a part of the larger ritual flow of the Sunday service. The classically-shaped Sunday service is, in effect, a drama in two acts: the *Service of the Word* and the *Service of the Table*. The Service of the Word, rooted in the synagogue, includes prayer, praise, the reading of Scripture, and preaching. The Service of the Table, rooted in the Upper Room, includes creed, offering, thanksgiving, and the Lord's Table. To move from the Service of the Word to the Service of the Table is to cross a boundary. The Service of the Word is done, figuratively at least, in a public place, and the whole world is invited to listen. At the Service of the Table, however, the curtain is symbolically drawn around the community of faith, for only the faithful can confess the creed and gather at the Table to participate in the body of Christ. On the boundary between the two services stands baptism, the act of initiation into the household of faith. Indeed, some liturgical traditions still pause at this boundary in worship to dismiss all of the nonbaptized. When they have passed through the waters of baptism, then they may enter into the new Canaan of the Lord's Table.

We can see something of this two-fold structure of worship in Luke's account of the two disciples on the road to Emmaus (24:13ff).[5] In fact, this story may well be shaped by the liturgical practice of the Lukan community. In the first part of the story, two disciples are trudging down the road from Jerusalem to the village of Emmaus, about seven miles away. The risen Christ joins them in their journey, but "their eyes were kept from recognizing him." The conversation among these disciples and Christ leads to this rather amazing verse:

And beginning with Moses and all the prophets, he interpreted

Boarding Pass

nwa. SKYTEAM

Name: HUBER/KEVIN   Confirmation #: 2Z6FMP   E-Ticket #: 012737552252

Date	Flight	From	To	Gate	Board	Depart	Arrive	Cabin	Seat
1 15Oct	NW233	Washington-Reagan	Detroit		1:53P	2:23P	4:01P	Coach	17-A
2 15Oct	NW1413	Detroit	Chicago		4:38P	5:08P	5:21P	Coach	15-D

Frequent Flyer #: Not Provided

Requests:

Remarks:

[Segment] Sec. Nr: [1] 88 [2] 28

Page 1 of 1

Bag Tag # NW535951

to them in all the scriptures the things concerning himself.
(Luke 24:27).

Now that is obviously rather extraordinary highway conversation. If we think liturgically, though, one could hardly
find a better one-sentence definition than this one of how the
early church viewed preaching. This is the sermon.

Now the story makes a shift. They arrive at the village,
and, at the urging of the disciples, the hidden Christ joins
them for a meal inside a house. Suddenly the guest becomes
the host, and the meal, described in clear eucharistic language, becomes an epiphany: "And their eyes were opened
and they recognized him."

One could not imagine a more powerful narrative depic-
tion of a Sunday worship service. Disciples walk down a public highway, hearing a sermon. Then they gather in the
privacy of a home for the sacred meal. The Service of the
Word and the Service of the Table. Moreover, they immediately sense the connection between the two experiences. The first
words spoken after the meal are, "Did not our hearts burn
within us while he talked to us on the road, while he opened
to us the scriptures?" (Luke 24:32).

When preaching is seen as a part of the overall drama of
worship, it is clearly the climax of the first act—but only of
the first act. When the service ends with a sermon and a
hymn, people are leaving the theater at intermission, and
missing the denouement of the drama. Preaching leads to the
second act, which is to say that preaching, liturgically speaking, is completed sacramentally. For those who are not part of
the household of faith, preaching urges toward baptism. For
those who are baptized, preaching builds up the body of
Christ and invites them once again to the Lord's Table. The
vision of justice seen at that Table strengthens and guides the
church in the world.

To view the act of preaching as embodied in the total service of worship should provide much comfort for preachers.
We are, among other things, relieved of the burden of carrying

the full weight of Sunday morning. I can remember a minister I encountered in my youth who felt the obligation, as he put it, "to preach the plan of salvation in every sermon, because someone out there in the pews may die tomorrow unsaved." I am convinced that this rather lachrymose version of evangelicalism has its more sophisticated counterparts in the form of preachers of all theological persuasions who share the common conviction that if anything substantive is to happen in worship, it will happen in the sermon.

The sermon is important, all right, but when the dramatic shape of the whole service is recognized, it becomes apparent that it is *all* of worship which proclaims the gospel. The service is a reenactment of salvation history, and the sermon is but a voice in the larger choir praising God for all that has been and will be.

This frees those of us who preach to take what we say in the pulpit with utmost seriousness, but also to shrug our shoulders in the recognition that what we say is always partial, temporary, and incomplete. When we preach, we are participating in the most important activity in which a human voice can engage—praising God. Yet we all remain stutterers and stammerers, perpetual amateurs in the very thing to which we have given our whole lives. But we need not worry. If our voices were to grow silent, as they eventually will, the very stones would cry out to the glory of God.

Notes

1. Paul Scherer, *The Word God Sent* (Grand Rapids: Baker Book House, 1965), 69.
2. Richard K. Fenn, *Liturgies and Trials* (New York: Pilgrim Press, 1982).
3. Anne Tyler, *Dinner at the Homesick Restaurant* (New York: Berkley Books, 1982), 21.
4. Fenn, *Liturgies and Trials*, 27.
5. *The Worshipbook* (Philadelphia: Westminster Press, 1972), 27.
6. The description of the trials of John the Baptist and Jesus appeared, in altered form, in Thomas G. Long, *Shepherds and Bathrobes* (Lima, Ohio: C.S.S. Press, 1987), 26–7.
7. Stanley Hauerwas, *A Community of Character: Toward a Constructive Christian Social Ethic* (Notre Dame: University of Notre Dame Press, 1981), 145–6.
8. Saint Augustine, *On Christian Doctrine*, trans. D.W. Robertson, Jr. (New York: The Liberal Arts Press, 1958), 142.
9. Georges Bernanos, *The Diary of a Country Priest*, trans. Pamela Morris (Garden City, NY: Doubleday and Co., 1974), 1–2.
10. William Muehl, *Why Preach? Why Listen?* (Philadelphia: Fortress Press, 1986), 39–40.

CHAPTER 2

1. F. Dean Leuking, *Preaching: The Art of Connecting God and People* (Waco, Texas: Word Books, 1985), 95.
2. This event, in a slightly different version, is described in Thomas G. Long, *Shepherds and Bathrobes* (Lima, Ohio: C.S.S. Press, 1987), 70–1.
3. Don S. Browning, *The Moral Context of Pastoral Care* (Philadelphia: Westminster Press, 1976).
4. As recorded in Robert McAfee Brown, "Light, Darkness, and Bridges in Norway," *The Christian Century* (January 7–14 1987): 5.
5. William Muehl, *Why Preach? Why Listen?* (Philadelphia: Fortress Press, 1986), 9.
6. *Ibid.*, 10.
7. John P. Meier, "Jesus Among the Historians," *The New York Times Book Review,* Sunday, 21 Dec. 1986, 1, 16–19.
8. *Ibid.*, 17.
9. *Ibid.*
10. *Ibid.*, 19.
11. *Ibid.*
12. Markus Barth, "Introduction," in Leonhard Goppelt, Helmut Thielicke, and Hans-Rudolf Muller-Schwefe, *The Easter Message Today,* trans. Salvator Attanasio and Darrell Likens Guder (New York: Thomas Nelson and Sons, 1964), 10–11.
13. *Ibid.*, 65.
14. Carl Braaten, "The Kingdom of God and Life Everlasting," in *Christian Theology: An Introduction to Its Traditions and Tasks,* ed. Peter C. Hodgson and Robert H. King (Philadelphia: Fortress Press, 1982), 279.
15. Hendrikus Berkhof, *Christian Faith: An Introduction to the Study of the Faith* (Grand Rapids, MI: Eerdmans, 1979), 312.
16. See, for example, Walter Sullivan, "Is There a Past in the Future?," *The New York Times,* 30 Dec. 1986, sec. C.
17. Jürgen Moltmann, *The Crucified God* (New York: Harper & Row, 1974), 178.

CHAPTER 3

1. Clyde Reid, *The Empty Pulpit* (New York: Harper & Row, 1967), 99.
2. Frederick Buechner, *Telling the Truth: The Gospel as Tragedy, Comedy, and Fairy Tale* (San Francisco: Harper & Row, 1977), 22–3.
3. Karl Barth, *The Word of God and the Word of Man* (New York: Harper & Row, 1928), 104–8.

4. Karl Barth, *Dogmatics in Outline,* trans. G. T. Thomson (New York: Harper Torchbooks, 1959), 142–3.
5. Fred B. Craddock, *Preaching* (Nashville: Abingdon Press, 1985), 44.
6. J. Randall Nichols, *Building the Word* (San Francisco: Harper & Row, 1980), 102–3.
7. Vance Barron, *Sermons for the Celebration of the Christian Year* (Nashville: Abingdon, 1977), 14.
8. Norman Vincent Peale, "Power Over All Your Difficulties," in *The Twentieth Century Pulpit,* ed. James W. Cox (Nashville: Abingdon Press, 1978), 167.
9. Anne Tyler, *Dinner at the Homesick Restaurant* (New York: Berkley Books, 1982), 291.
10. See the discussion of Lakoff's work in Deborah Tannen, *Conversational Style: Analyzing Talk Among Friends* (Norwood, New Jersey: Ablex Publishing Co., 1984), 14.
11. John Fry, "Blindness," in *The Twentieth Century Pulpit, Volume II,* ed. James W. Cox (Nashville: Abingdon Press, 1981), 74–5.
12. Virgil P. Elizondo, "A Child in a Manger. . . ." in *Proclaiming the Acceptable Year,* ed. Justo L. Gonzalez (Valley Forge, PA: Judson Press, 1982), 64.
13. See the discussion of this research in Tannen, *Conversational Style,* 26–7.

CHAPTER 4

1. Geoffrey Wainwright, *Doxology: The Praise of God in Worship, Doctrine, and Life* (New York: Oxford University Press, 1980), 8.
2. See the discussion of this phrase in William H. Willimon, *The Service of God: How Worship and Ethics Are Related* (Nashville: Abingdon Press, 1983), 15–19.
3. Lesslie Newbigin, *Foolishness to the Greeks* (Grand Rapids, MI: William B. Eerdmans Publishing Co., 1986), 150.
4. Annie Dillard, *Teaching a Stone to Talk* (New York: Harper & Row, 1982), 19–20.
5. For a more complete analysis of this passage, see Thomas G. Long, "Reclaiming the Unity of Word and Sacrament in Presbyterian and Reformed Worship," *Reformed Liturgy and Music,* vol. XVI, no. 1 (Winter, 1982): 12–17.

Printed in the United States
20426LVS00001B/127